ALTARcation

My Story of Forgiveness After a Broken Engagement

Ericka McCracken

Copyright Page

Table of Contents:

Dedication

First and foremost, I want to thank you God for my past, my present and the great future you have already set up for me. I know that everything I have been through has been an opportunity to testify about Your goodness. Your peace and presence have kept me on days when I did not have the strength to see past my circumstances. I pray that I have made You proud Father with this opportunity to witness to others about Your goodness and grace. You've never left me and I know You never will.

Mommy
What can I say to the strongest woman I know? As a young girl, I always knew that if I could be half the woman you are, I would be successful in life. You've taught me what it means to roll with the punches that life may bring your way. You have also taught me what it means to take care of a home, be a great wife and mother as well as what it truly means to be selfless. I pray you know what your sacrifices have meant to me and Eb, and that you will always be my "Shero."

Daddy
Daddy, I thank you for the sacrifices you've made to create a better life for Eb and I. I know it could not have been easy. As a woman, I now understand how your choices have blessed me and still do to this day. You raised us the best way you knew how and for that, I will forever be grateful.

Sissy

How did my little sissy become my big sister? I have watched you mature from a quiet and reserved lady to a superb wife and mother. I look up to you more than you know and cannot wait to see what God has in store for you and your very own growing family. Thank you for always having my back, front and everything in between and being one of my biggest supporters and cheerleaders. You always know what to say to make me feel better and your wisdom about life has blessed me so much. Keep shining and always remember, I'm still your big sister!

Dinner Crew

Who would have thought our friendship would surpass our time spent in Nelson Farms, Bethel High School, UVa and now to Atlanta. We have been through so much together and I know if I ever need a good laugh or cry, I can always count on you. Thanks for being "my village" and blessing me beyond what words could express. I love you ladies. Know that my life would not be what it is without your presence, support and your cooking every Wednesday and Sunday.

RJ

Thank you for teaching me what it means to truly love and forgive. Experiences should build our character and help us grow to new heights. Our relationship has taught me just that.

Lindsey Huth

Thank you so much Soror for your contribution to my book. Your words spoke to me and truly embodied what this memoir is all about.

Justin Hart

Justin, you have been such a huge catalyst in helping me complete this book. Thank you for encouraging me every step of the way. Your knowledge and willingness to not sacrifice quality for anything has aided me in making this memoir reach its fullest potential.

Mary Hoekstra

Mary, you have been more of a blessing than you realize. Thank you for your contribution to this memoir as an editor and as a friend. Most importantly, your quirky sense of humor. It's contagious.

Nicole Gray

Thank you for your vision for the graphics of ALTARcation. Your talent is beyond measure. I'm so thankful to call you my sister.

My Legacy Team

Jamie and Nastassja, thank you for believing in me and helping me build the legacy that will surpass my life. You all have challenged, motivated, supported, and most importantly, loved me and for that, I am eternally grateful.

Readers of *ALTARcation*

Yes readers, I thank you. You could have read anything in the world and yet, you decided to support me. Thank you for allowing me to share my experiences and prayerfully, if you are going through this now, you know you are not alone. If you have been through it, you are healing each and every day. Remember, Romans 5:3-5:

"Not only so, but we also rejoice in our sufferings, because we know that suffering produces perseverance; perseverance, character; and character, hope. And hope does not disappoint us, because God has poured out his love into our hearts by the Holy Spirit, whom he has given us." Thank you, Thank you, Thank you.

Hold On by Lindsey Huth

1. Hold on
2. Keep breathing
3. Don't cry
4. Stay strong

We all have steps, strategies, methods, mechanisms to cope with the pain
We hold on to the pieces of ourselves we still recognize
Keep breathing
Don't cry
Stay strong

The world passes us by, never stopping to ask what's wrong, time stops for no one
So we hold on to the pieces of ourselves we still recognize
Keep telling ourselves it's not as bad as it could be
Don't Cry
Stay Strong

Your friends start to see that something is different about you. You can't bear to look them in the eyes anymore. What if they saw the part of you that you've been hiding from yourself?
So, we hold on to the pieces of ourselves we still recognize
Keep telling ourselves it's not as bad as it could be
Don't let them see too much of who we are
Stay strong

The stitches holding up the smiles on our faces get weighed down by everything we aren't saying and unexpressed emotions eat at our souls like acid laced poison

But we…
Hold on to the pieces of ourselves we still recognize
Keep telling ourselves it's not as bad as it could be
Don't let them see too much of who we are
Stay standing

Hold on; Keep breathing. Don't cry. Stay strong. Stay.
Stay. Keep breathing. Hold on. Don't cry. Stay strong.
Keep telling yourself, stay strong, keep breathing.
So we hold on to keep telling ourselves stay strong
Keep breathing
If we can just stay standing
Hold on

But I
can't
anymore
I can't, hold on anymore
I can't, feel my fingers
My lungs can't breathe anymore,
I'm choking on the bloody truth I've been biting my tongue
to keep in
I don't think I can hold back the tears anymore
The dam I've plastered over my eyes won't hold anymore
Where is the girl that knew how to stay strong evermore?

I had a strategy, a method a mechanism, a way of living
with the pain.

But little by little everything I had ever known shattered
into broken pieces in between my fingers, there was
nothing left to hold on to anymore so…

So I let go
Every breath reminded me of what I didn't want to be

So for a moment I held my breath and didn't take in more of the negativity. I shut out the air of the people poisoning me
I let go
Quit breathing
Looking into the eyes of people I'd never met before looked like mirrors showing me everything I didn't want them to see in me and finally rain drop sized tears rolled down the cliffs of my high cheek bones and the emotions danced across my face like the wind of a hurricane
I let go
Quit breathing
Stopped holding back the tears

I grew up in a house full of warriors. I ate my emotions with each meal and learned how to stand up straight and hit back harder
Through hell and high water I just kept standing
Until the day when
I let go
Quit breathing
Stopped holding back the tears
Found myself broken on my knees with nowhere to look but up

And down here
Where I never thought I supposed to be
I found you
And through you I found me
I finally felt free

You saw me when I didn't want to be seen and you
Loved me when I didn't want to be loved, and you
Kept me when all I wanted to do was run

You had a strategy, a method, a way to wash away the pain

Even when I lost all the broken pieces of who I thought I was
You held on to who you know I am meant to be

You never stopped holding on to me

When I spit your love back at you because it didn't taste like anything familiar to a tongue full of lies and I choked on your mercy through a throat lined with of all the things I said I'd never do
You still remembered to breathe for me
You kept breathing so I didn't have to

The people on bicycles that tried to sell religion at my doorstep always said that God is love,
but they don't tell you that loving God doesn't guarantee love from others
When they asked me who I was now and if I thought I could be all innocent now and they told me I couldn't stop being who I was just because I wanted to and they said I was such a waste of the hip-hop rap lyric they made me out to be
And when I told them it wasn't true
And when I showed them it was
While I was learning what it meant to be imperfect yet still enough
You placed peace in tears that filled my pillow each night
You taught me that it is okay to cry for everything that happened
And those tears don't mean I'm not strong, only that I'm human

I was taught never to be a doormat, not a tool or a trophy. A woman doesn't need a man nor does any one individual need another. Be strong. Use the pain of your misery to weld a stronger backbone. Just keep moving. You don't *need* anyone
We all need someone

We all fall sometimes
To be weak is to be human and we cannot do all things
alone
You promised to be my strength
You are the strength that lives within me

You held on
Kept breathing
Showed me a piece of myself I didn't recognize
You stay strong

And I am learning to love myself because you first loved
me
I'm not sure I've found out how to forgive myself for
everything just yet
But you promised to never leave me
And for the first time in my life and I believe you

So now I have a strategy, a mechanism, a way to move past
the pain

1. Hold onto you
2. Keep praying
3. Release pain and joy through tears when I need to
4. Stay standing in grace and love and peace

I'm free

Prelude

"It is better to light a candle than curse the darkness." Peter Benenson, Founder of Amnesty International, December 10, 1961.

Darkness has long been a metaphor for ignorance or evil. The Bible contains hundreds of references to darkness, referring either to the period of ignorance before the realization of faith (that is, prior to 'seeing the light'), death, or to the Devil (The Prince of Darkness); for example, in Romans 13:11-12: And that, knowing the time, that now it is high time to awake out of sleep: for now is our salvation nearer than when we believed. The night is far spent, the day is at hand: let us therefore cast off the works of darkness, and let us put on the armor of light.

I came across this quote when I read that Nate Berkus, of the "The Nate Berkus Show," and "Oprah's Big Give," had recently become engaged and had been re-telling the story of how his previous partner had been killed in the Tsunami of 2004. Berkus described the heartache that he endured at the loss of his partner. After mourning his loss, he faced a difficult choice and had used the aforementioned quote to make that choice. And it just hit me! If he could rebound after such a traumatic ordeal, I *could* get through what was happening in my life. Losing a loved one is never easy, and while my ex-fiancé RJ had not passed away, I was truly mourning the death of our relationship. Like Berkus, I chose to light a candle in the darkness, knowing that it wouldn't be dark forever.

Wait, "Scandal" is on

I can't believe my ears. I must be confused. I know he didn't just say, "let's put our engagement on hold." We were nearly five months in. Our wedding date and venue were already confirmed. My wedding dress had already been purchased. In three weeks, I was scheduled to meet with a potential caterer. You put shoes on hold, maybe a coat, and even a phone call. Not a wedding....not our wedding....my wedding!

This can't be right. I was just there, less than 12 hours ago, in sunny California. The weather had been beautiful and everything had been so serene. I had even ventured out to the local mall and bought an outfit for our engagement photos. I remember RJ didn't seem too enthused when I showed it to him, but I just figured he was hungry. After all, we just started "The Daniel Fast," which meant we were not to eat foods that weren't natural and through the Fast, we would gain spiritual clarity. Both of us desired to gain clarity about how to proceed with where we were going to live, and which of us would have to move, since we lived on different Coasts. It had seemed so right to participate together in the Fast. This was my second time participating in this Fast, but it was RJs first, and I knew it would be difficult for him. Maybe that was the reason for his lack of enthusiasm about my new outfit. What I didn't know was that my world would be shattered as I drove back home after leaving him, or rather him leaving me.

I parked my car in the garage. I just sat there; I couldn't move. My heart was beating so fast, and all I could think was, "Not again! God, what did I do to deserve this-this time?" I was prayerful and hopeful about our future; I was practicing abstinence; I felt like I was doing all of the right things this time around; but I still ended up in the same predicament.

Yes, you read it correctly, "same predicament." You see, at this same time last year, to the day, I was going through a break-up that nearly broke me to my core. Same

Daniel Fast, same day, what could this mean? During that break up, I was very reflective about everything. I knew there was a bigger purpose for me, for us, even though I couldn't see it at the time. I didn't really ask, "Why me," but I did ask the Lord how I could learn from that crushing ending.

This time, with RJ, I wasn't so optimistic. To be honest, I was beginning to feel like I was cursed. I didn't feel I had the strength to get through this experience again. We were in the middle of planning our wedding. No one ever told me that engagements don't turn into weddings. Truth be told, that was furthest from my mind, despite the struggle we had on who would move. He lived in Los Angeles and I lived in Atlanta. Neither one of us wanted to uproot ourselves and make that move, even for love. Regardless, we didn't have a stressful relationship. What was happening to us doesn't happen to "normal" people who love each other. People who have known each other for nearly half of their lives, especially if no one was cheating or lying to the other. That stuff happens on reality shows and can even be seen on your favorite court shows. But not us.

We were solid.

Or so I thought.

RJ's and I relationship was not stressful, but it was definitely not perfect either. In fact, we were close to never having a romantic relationship at all. I was very hesitant to give RJ another chance at love because I felt he could never fully commit to me. Whether it was distance or his desire to become a successful actor, I felt that RJ had priorities; I just was not one of them. That all changed in 2011, after his trip to Atlanta, where I live. RJ confessed then that he actually wanted to begin a romantic relationship with me, after we had been friends for so long. Despite the significant geographical distance between us, and our living on two different coasts, he wanted us to be together. I have to admit, at first, I was extremely hesitant; I had heard it before. However, this time, there was no "but," in regards to why it couldn't workout. It was just him believing that we had to start somewhere. Two months later, I was taking my first visit to California to spend time with him, and that had turned into a surprise proposal in Malibu.

As I thought about that day, the only word that I could think of was, "lies." RJ on one knee, in the sand, on the beach, saying he loved me and wanted to spend the rest of his life with me. Lies. As I mulled that over, all I could see was fire red. I was angry, which is usually my first emotion when I'm upset. When I looked down at my ring finger, I didn't know what to feel anymore. I wanted to take that ring off and throw it in the drain behind my house, but I knew that wasn't going to happen. It cost too much money. I was upset, but definitely not stupid. I did, however, want to snatch that ring off my finger. I felt I was living a lie, but I knew deep down, I did not want it to be over yet. I wasn't ready. I was fearful that if I took the ring off, I would not be able to put it back on. Despite what RJ did and said the night he asked to put our wedding on hold, I wasn't ready to give up and declare our relationship dead. I felt it could be revived but I didn't know how to do that, or what to do. The one thing I was sure of was that I did not deserve this. No one does.

When issues arise in my life, I reflect on the history of them, so I began to rethink our relationship and how we got to this point. We had been through a lot in a friendship that first developed when we were in 6th grade, but canceling our wedding hadn't occurred to me. (I'll touch more on RJ's and my history in a later chapter, but just know it began when both of us were extremely young.)

As I reflected back through the weekend, what enraged me more than what he said was that I had just been with him. We were literally face-to-face hours ago. We could have had that conversation when we were in the same place and we had the ability to actually look into each other's eyes. I had to wonder, if that had been the scenario, would there have been a different result? I will never know, but I do know that at the time, I felt like he was a coward for waiting until I got home to hit me with one of the biggest bombshells of my life.

That's the honest to God truth. I lost a lot of respect for him for a while, but after some time passed, I re-evaluated why he may have decided to handle it that way. I'm sure it was probably just as hard for him to do, as it was for me to have it done. It didn't hit me until I was talking with a guy I was dating at the time, as well as watching "Iyanla" and tearing up, that I discovered the level of pain the "hurter" inflicts on the "hurtee."

I know the jargon may be throwing you off, but don't lose me here. Breaking up is one of the hardest things to do, whether that other "hurtee" person deserved it or not. I realized then that RJ probably had made one of the hardest decisions he had ever made. Telling the woman you proposed to that you might have made a mistake could not have been easy for him. Especially without being able to console me, or see the reaction on my face. While I might have handled it differently, I realized that there was nothing cowardly about it. In fact, RJ having the courage to express himself was more courageous than I originally thought.

"Can we talk?" My sister said those three words to me, and I dreaded hearing them just like men do. After about a week of reeling about being in limbo during my engagement, and not knowing how things would work out, my sister came to my house before dinner at our friend's house. After a few moments of casual talk, she sat me down. From the look on her face, I knew it was serious. I knew what those three words meant. Those three words made me forget about the Daniel Fast I was still on and divert all of my attention to her. I walked over and pulled out the bar chair that was beside her, and I sat down. Initially, she just looked at me. She reached out for my hand and her eyes began to well up.

"You deserve someone who knows they want to marry you." As tears streamed from her eyes, I knew she was right. My eyes began to fill with tears too. That set off a light bulb in me. She said a few things after that, but her first sentence was all I needed to hear. As her lips were moving, so were the thoughts in my head. For some odd reason, I felt renewed. Rejuvenated. The pain I had been feeling for the last few days left, and I knew what I had to do.

The next day, I still carried that same feeling of renewal. I went to work, had training that afternoon, and it actually felt like a typical Thursday. The week before, I had felt like I was in such a dark haze. The Thursday normality was just what I needed. The sun kissed my brown skin that day as I smiled to the guards who greeted me at the door as I entered my job. I laughed with co-workers and forgot about my troubles. RJ kept calling me, but I didn't care to answer. I didn't care what he wanted in that moment. All I knew was what I needed.

I was prepared that night when RJ and I finally spoke. I was unsure if he was still on the fence, but I had a glimmer of hope that he had experienced the same epiphany I had. He knew what he wanted and realized that it was me. Despite how encouraged and empowered I felt at the time, deep down, I knew this could go either way. This may be our last conversation and our relationship could be over. What I also knew was that this limbo feeling I had couldn't go on another day. After I called RJ and we got the niceties out of the way such as discussing how our day went, I asked him had he made a decision about whether to proceed with our engagement or not.

I told him bluntly, "I deserve someone who is 150% sure that he wants to marry me. If you can't say that, we just need to cut our ties now." This is it, I thought. The moment of truth. He will step up and make his commitment to me once again, but this time, for good.

Wait for it.

Wait for it.

Then, the unthinkable happened.

Nothing.

Nothing happened.

You read it right, nothing. He had nothing to add. Didn't fight for me like I wished he would, but deep down I knew he wouldn't. In his eyes, if he fought for me, he would then be giving up on his acting career. I knew that wasn't an option in his mind. As he headed to his workshop in Los Angeles and I sat on my couch in Atlanta, I knew we were more than just on different coasts; we were in two different spaces mentally. I couldn't believe it. The engagement was off. We were done. My dream was deferred and, at the time, it didn't seem THAT bad. I walked upstairs and proceeded to call my sister. I told her what happened and I could tell she breathed a sigh of relief.

I knew that she was happy that I chose being true to myself rather than waiting for validation from someone who was unsure of what he wanted. As I actually said to her, "We're done Eb," out loud, I began to weep. She offered to come over. It was late and I didn't feel like much company.

I opened the drawer on my nightstand. I searched frantically for the box the ring came in and once I found it, my eyes locked in on it. As I looked at my left hand, I knew it was real. I carefully glided the ring off of my finger and placed it in the box I had searched so feverishly for. I sat on my bed for about thirty seconds, trying to take in everything that just happened, when I looked at the time and realized it was a few minutes after 10 pm.

I had no more time for tears. "Scandal" was on. I watched the episode and had a good night's sleep. I was the gladiator that night.

Everyone always laughs when I tell them that once "Scandal" came on, the tears stopped rolling and I was immediately glued to the TV. Most of America knows about "Scandal" and has followed the story line for months, but was it *really* that good? I couldn't tell you what happened on that particular episode but to me, it was the best diversion. When I think about it now, it allowed me not to think about my situation and be engaged in someone else's instead. Someone's situation that was a little worse than mine. The love triangle that Olivia Pope was in had me so engaged that I actually think I did forget what had just happened to me.

My life had just changed forever and you wouldn't have been able to tell by the way I was acting. Forget Kerry Washington. I should have won the Emmy that night for best actress in a drama. My award was uninterrupted sleep. I slept like a baby and woke up feeling better than I had all week.

You see, one minute you are crying and the next minute you are laughing. It's so weird, but it may be your reality for a while. The next day, I felt even stronger than the day before. I told my boss what happened, and for the next few hours I was good. My boss tried to defend RJ, like he usually did the men in my life, but there was nothing he could say that day. The "Shelf Theory" is what he proclaimed RJ was using. The "Shelf Theory" can be described as what occurs when a man or woman puts you on a theoretical shelf until they are ready to be with you completely. My boss's rationale was that RJ was placing me on the shelf and when he was ready, he would come back for me. Until RJ was in a situation where he was comfortable with his career, he couldn't pursue me with 100% of his heart. Malarkey huh? I didn't understand his perspective at the time and didn't want too. He wasn't going to take away the peace I felt at that time. Too bad it wouldn't be long before my peace was disturbed.

I left my boss's office later to call RJ and discuss how we planned to handle the commitments we had already made for the wedding, and how to dissolve the bank account we had already opened up. I almost lasted the entire conversation without becoming emotional, until we discussed having to cancel our venue. That was the nail in the coffin. It was real. I knew they would have questions as to why. As I sat in my car and made the phone call to the venue, I bravely requested that the room be cancelled.

"Why?" she asked. "Is there something wrong with the venue?" The water works began to flow, "No, there will not be a wedding" I responded.

She took a breath and said, "*There's* a reason to cancel."

I could tell she was not trying to be facetious. She was trying to divert from the real problem. I asked about the cancellation procedures and how much we would have to forfeit. She gave me the specifics and I ended the call.

To make matters worse, it was a little gloomy outside when I made that call, so it just felt like a bad day all around at that point. I decided, while I was out there, I might as well see if I could return the wedding dress I had purchased nearly two months prior. I called David's Bridal and politely asked about their return policy. She asked for my name, which pulled up the wedding name and date. She asked me why I wanted to return the dress and told me that I could exchange it for another one. I informed her that the wedding was canceled, and nearly broke down. I believe she could hear it in my voice. She asked me to hold while she spoke to the manager. When she returned, she told me that I could exchange it, and she almost sounded like she wanted to weep for me. My eyes began to fill with tears again and I knew my co-workers would see me in the car, so I hurried back into the building, then nearly ran to the bathroom as quickly as I could. As I entered the women's restroom, I walked towards the back locker room and just wept. I stayed in that bathroom for about thirty minutes. I knew I couldn't go directly back to work because my face was still puffy and my eyes were red. I decided to stay for another thirty minutes. After I pulled myself together, I saw a co-worker as I was exiting the restroom and even laughed for a bit.

Cry. Laugh. Get familiar with it.

If someone video-taped my life, they would think I was a complete lunatic. Who does that? Cries for an hour and walks into their co-worker's office like nothing ever happened. Why didn't I just stay home for the day? Honestly, that thought never crossed my mind. I knew that would do nothing but cause me to think about it more and become sadder or even depressed about it. Did I have the right? Probably. It just isn't in my DNA to do that. I'll call it "Superwoman Syndrome," in which SHE can do all, and be all, to everyone, regardless of her condition or circumstances. Blame my mother. (I'll touch on that later too, but all I know how to do is to keep moving.) "Business as usual" is my motto in times of crisis. It probably isn't the best way, but at the time, it was the only way I knew. In my eyes, I had moped long enough. Time to get on with the rest of my life. I think that is what "Scandal" represented to me; getting back into the routine that I would normally do.

I feel normality is so important in the healing process. It also reminds us that life still moves on. "Scandal" was not going to wait until I felt good enough to watch it to come back on ABC. I firmly believe that getting back to your normal routine is almost therapeutic in the healing process. But there are rules. Acknowledging the hurt is vital in the healing process, so I don't want to ignore that part. I am not the prototype for how to heal, but I try to ensure that, as quickly as I can, I get back to what feels normal, and that helps me confirm that life will be "normal" for me again. Reading this is a good step in that direction. I'm not just saying this because I wrote the book.

Well maybe a little, but it demonstrates the steps you are going to take to heal. Everyone's journey is different so just know that it is indeed that, a journey. The way you come out of this is also in your hands. If nothing else, know that this moment in your life doesn't *define* you, it *refines* you. Thank you for taking the time to read my story, my truth. May it bless you to read it, as it has blessed me   to   be   able   to   write   it.

ALTARcation

Chapter 1
Mirror, Mirror

I can't type another sentence without letting you know something vital. This is not a book with all the answers. This is my experience. I hope you gain something from reading this, but please know that you won't find all your answers here.

If you find a book that claims it does have all your answers, RUN! QUICK! Don't just place the book down, throw it on the ground and stomp on it like it was on fire. Jump as high as you can and come down on that book like it's a giant cockroach in your kitchen. There is only one book in the world with all the answers and that's the Bible. Any other book is a fraud.

Whew. Okay. Got that out the way. Now we can move on.

My hope for this book is that it makes you aware that other people in the world (unfortunately) are experiencing the same thing you are. Breaking off an engagement is one of the loneliest feelings that I've ever felt. You go from nearly sealing a covenant that makes you one with someone else, to just being alone. As ironic as it sounds, it is our current reality. I have to also remind you that this feeling isn't going to last always. For now, though, we *must* feel this. We *must* endure this. I think that's one of the most important nuggets of advice I received. It is to just feel whatever it is that you are feeling. You will either feel it now or you'll feel it later. Personally, I'd rather take mine now.

That being said, there are a few rules that I do believe are quintessential to helping you pick up the pieces after a break-up. I know they have helped me through this experience and they have helped countless others, but like I stated earlier, your experience is exactly that, yours.

I pray that this book finds you where you are and then elevates you to new heights. This journey will have valleys and peaks, but it is guaranteed to make you stronger if you understand that all you can do is take one step at a time. Healing will take its course, if you allow it to. I truly believe the saying, "What doesn't kill you makes you stronger." I know it sounds cliché. I know you are probably rolling your eyes right now. I know you think this is like every other book that you have read. Well, it's not. There are still some things that will always ring true. This is one of them.

Superwoman Syndrome

As I write this book, I realize how hard this whole process is going to be. I mean, being vulnerable is tough. I must say, it is something I have always tried to shy away from. Growing up and seeing my mother handle difficulties and issues, I've learned that the show always "went on." Let me clarify a bit. Regardless of what she went through, business was always taken care of. One moment in particular sticks out to me. When my uncle passed away when I was in middle school, it was the first time in my life I recall my mother ever crying. When I saw my mom crying, I didn't know what to do. I wanted to console her, but I didn't know how. What was I to do when my hero is

32

hurting? I relegated myself back to my room, while my dad gave her a hug, and my mom called my school to let them know my sister and I would be missing school that week. I vividly remember Mom nearly breaking down when she was speaking to the school counselor. She didn't say much, but tears just streamed from her eyes. She shook her head a few times but managed to keep her composure. I don't know what was being said on the other end of the phone, but I believe my counselor was telling my mother what needed to happen with school for my sister and I.

Mom wiped her eyes, pulled out a pen and pad, and jotted down notes. She said thanks and hung up the phone. Taking charge as she usually did, and does, she told my sister and I what needed to happen that week for school and we listened. At that moment, I knew my mother was what society would now identify as a boss. You see, my mom didn't wear butt-length weaves or gold chains. She wasn't "balling" out of control with stacks of money, but she was definitely in control. Regardless of what was going on, she made sure her children and her household was taken care of. Nothing was lacking, despite the unfortunate circumstances of my uncle's death. She knew, once we returned home, life would go on and she wanted to make sure home was taken care of first. She has always had that mentality and as far as I can remember, she's always been a boss. I saluted her only using my eyes and actions that day. To me, she was, and still is, the epitome of what a true, grown woman is.

Okay, so things change sometimes. Nowadays, my mother cries at the drop of hat. They are all tears of joy now, whether it's a card for Mother's Day or a sweet gesture of providing her favorite coffee. All the tears she didn't use during my adolescence seemed to have been stored for times like that. Oddly enough, my mother didn't cry at my sister's and my graduation, or at my sister's wedding. I think she cried because she always knew those things would happen. She had no doubt about our potential and what our achievements would be.

I think what makes my mother most proud of her children are the things she didn't teach us, but we inherited from her. Her willingness to give, regardless of what she has, or the love that even my sister and I have for each other. My mother is more proud of the women we are than anything we've ever achieved. Despite my mother's tears now, it is extremely hard for me to show that vulnerability to others. I feel like I have to be that "hero" that my mother is. To be frank, it's not a true representation of my feelings. In fact, I now think it demonstrates that nothing affects me which is farthest from the truth. I hurt like you hurt. I cry like you cry, but for the longest time, I thought crying displayed weakness. This experience has taught me that weakness or what I would rather call my "area of improvement" is actually not showing emotion or vulnerability. Feeling that showing emotion is not necessary is the bigger issue for me.

Channel Your Energy

Switching gears, one of my dreams in life is to be a documentarian. I know it will come to pass. I love to tell stories, especially those from tragedy to triumph, of faith and perseverance. Many of us can watch Netflix all day and binge on the many documentaries that are available to view. I truly believe documentaries are a secret way to educate people while entertaining them at the same time. We learn so much about different issues, cultures, and perspectives by watching documentaries, whether they are on subjects that intrigue or disgust us.

I named my production company, "My Legacy," because I want the work I do to outlive me. For years to come, I want my work to be something that society, especially women, can relate to. Quality is what is most important to me. With that being said, I do partake in reality television too. It's hard not to, in this day and age. As I was watching "Love and Hip Hop New York" (Don't judge me!), Tahari, the previous girlfriend of a famous rapper, Joe Budden played a track for him that discussed their tumultuous relationship, and the hurt he had caused her throughout the years. Their turbulent relationship was now available for the world to hear in a four-minute song. As the track played, Tahari looked gratified, like she got everything out. Her emotions, her feelings, I envied that. The look on her face said it all. Not that I wanted to look like her, but I wanted to feel that same gratification.

As much as I talked about everything with God and my sis, I felt like I needed to really release it in an artistic way. My next thought was, "How?" I wasn't a singer or a rapper. I couldn't go to the studio to lay down tracks. How could I release my emotions was the question that I asked myself on a consistent basis for a few months. My pain, my anger, and ultimately my joy? I mean, I thought I was pretty artistic. I *am* a writer.

I WRITE!

Bingo!

After confiding in God, my friends, and my counselor, I decided to start documenting my feelings so that I could retrieve them when I was ready to create something that would encompass this period in my life. I had to determine what platform I would use. I wasn't sure if a fiction story was appropriate, or a screenplay. The more I pondered the idea, the more I knew a memoir, would be best. As hard as it was, I knew it was something I had to do, not only for myself, but also for so many others who are, or were, or may be, in the same predicament I was in. I realized the need for a memoir even more when I looked for books to help me deal with my emotions and feelings during this time. I didn't find many. I only found one that spoke to me about a news reporter in Atlanta whose fiancé called off the wedding during the rehearsal dinner. I know, right? Low, low, low down.

Her book touched on faith and forgiveness, which really helped me know I wasn't alone. I reached out to her and she gave me pointers on my next steps and congratulated me on the courage I had to embark on this journey.

I challenge you to reach into your creative side -- and trust me, you have one. Whether it is dancing, singing, photography, or spoken word, find that creative side and release it. There is nothing more rewarding than turning your pain into pleasure in the sense of completing a product in a constructive, creative way. During my last break up, I created a web series and even produced five episodes that are currently on YouTube. I now have something tangible that resulted from a dark period in my life. I guess you could say I turned my lemons into lemonade; pretty sweet lemonade at that.

My sister, as well as my sorority sister, told me that I should channel my experiences while they were raw, while I was living it. I knew that I had a story worth sharing, but I am an extremely private person when it comes to expressing myself to people I don't know, especially in regard to my personal life. Facebook and Twitter rants about how annoyed I am about people, places, and things, are something that I just don't do. They provide great entertainment to me but they're something I just never really felt were successful in working through an issue. I knew that I needed to share what I had been through to more than just those close to me. Millions of women (and men) have faced this issue, and I knew that healing was something many were searching for. I had to give these women hope. I had to let them know that while it hurts, we will move on and be stronger because of it.

We will get married.

We aren't damaged goods.

We aren't rejects.

Someone loves us. God loves us and so will another man, the right man, our husband.

It will be a love like we've never known.

Prayer

Initially, I released my feelings through prayer. I knew that even though God didn't respond to me verbally, He heard me and understood my pain. I was uninterrupted and I didn't feel that if I said the wrong thing, I would be punished. Spending time with God became more and more natural to me. Within the past few years, my relationship with God changed, and I realized just how vital He was to my life. I used to only go to God when I was in pain or in need, thinking I could handle everything else on my own. It wasn't long before I realized that I needed God day and night, 24/7, 365, and I wouldn't allow my circumstances to determine my praise. It took years to get to that point but I'm thankful I did. When this situation arose, I knew that, just like the day before, I would call on God and I knew He would be there, as always.

Wherever you are in your faith, whether you are a regular churchgoer or only go on holidays, continue to cultivate your relationship with God. The relationship with Him is most important to your life, in your healing and peace. Imagine calling your best girlfriend and he/she is always available, never too busy to listen to your issues, always available to help you face the day ahead. God is that, and more than you could fathom. He's the only one I know who is *always* available and will never be too busy for me. There are certain things in life that people, or yourself, can't handle alone, because trust me, if it were true, I would have known. Give God a chance to be your first resort. You won't be sorry.

Change Your Scene

I did what any heartbroken women would do next. No, not bust the windows out his car. I talked to my closest friend, my sister. She and I are identical twins, so for those of you who are an identical twin, or know identical twins, you know how strong that bond is. My sister continued being a great sister to me, talking and encouraging me like I knew she would. She and her husband allowed me to spend a week at their home after everything happened, so I could clear my head and just get away. I appreciated that time away, and having company that would get my mind off of everything. If you have someone who wouldn't mind you coming by for a few days, or however long you need, reach out to them. I know God places people on earth to help us with whatever we are going through. The experience of a break-up, more than anything, is the time to utilize them. Don't sit in your house, depressed and lonely. Find those you are closest with and ask them for whatever you may need. I'm sure that whatever you need (within reason) they would be happy to oblige you. I'm blessed that I have a sister who is local, and who will help me. Even if it's just leaving for the weekend to visit a friend to clear your head, do it. After that week away, I returned to my home with a renewed sense of self. RJ didn't live with me so I didn't have much memorabilia of him, or things we had done, around the house but if that is your case, please take a few days to grieve. The reprieve will help you out immensely in the long run.

Once I sat down at my computer with random notes that I jotted down about specific feelings and events, I had to put them all together. Where would I begin? I hadn't outlined chapters or even thought of a title, but knew I would piece my thoughts and feelings together and watch God work. I immediately began to think of all the conversations I'd had with people over the last few months.

Some were happy, some were sad, some were angry, and some were peaceful.

Earlier, I talked about whether you are the victim or the victor. I'm not going to school you like a teacher would her students, but I want you to keep this in the back of your mind. It is something that you must continually remind yourself about, because it is easy to slip back into "victim mode." This can especially be easy when you have to retell your story. Your girlfriends can get you fired up, making you feel like your ex is the scum of the earth. You may even get mad about things that you weren't initially mad at. That's when you must stop. You must reassess and revaluate where your headspace is.

A single conversation can bring you back from a place of deliverance. Don't let anyone steal your joy. That doesn't always mean making you sad, but it also means making you angry. After breakups, I was infamous for amping my friends up. I would get them angry and have them thinking of things that they may not have even thought of before. I was the hype woman to my friend's story sound track. Not until recently did I realize the effect that had on my friends and their relationships. I remember one incident in particular, where my sister was telling me a story, and she just wanted to vent, and I made her rehash everything all over again. I even encouraged her to confront her boyfriend at the time, and once we got off the phone, immediately, I knew I had done something wrong. I realized just how powerful my words are.

Ladies, I tell you from experience, if you have a friend or you are that friend, keep quiet. If you have a friend, realize how much you should tell them, and be firm in not allowing them to make comments or steal your peace. If you are that friend, stop what you are doing.

Really, stop it.

Realize the power of your words and make sure you are using the right ones, at the right time, and for the right reasons. If your words are not encouraging your friends, don't say them. We live in a society now where "keeping it real" or "keeping it 100" are the mottoes to live by. The scripture, Romans 12:2 states, "Don't copy the behavior and customs of this world, but let God transform you into a new person by changing the way you think. Then you will learn to know God's will for you, which is good, pleasing and perfect."

We have to get out of the mindset that to be truthful is to be brutal. Honesty never has to be brutal, just from the heart.

Chapter 2

My First Dance

This was supposed to be the event of the year for 11th graders, the Ring Dance. My dress was purchased, I'd bought my shoes; hair and nail appointments scheduled AND I had a date, a college sophomore who was often compared to Ginuwine, the singer. He had light skin, pearly white teeth, and wavy hair that would make you seasick by looking at it. In actuality, he was about six inches shorter than Ginuwine but you get my drift. I told all my friends and even those who weren't, about my boyfriend, who's coming down from college to escort me. From college.... for me! While the girls oooh'd and the boys scrunched up their faces, I knew that everyone wanted to see who this mystery guy was. Unbeknownst to me, they would never get the chance.

About 11am that morning, my stud college beau would cancel escorting me to the dance, over email. You read it right. It was the early 2000's and neither one of us had a cell phone, so I guess it was an acceptable form of communication. I may be overly dramatic here, but you never really expect to be dumped over your Hotmail account for the Ring Dance, which was equivalent to the senior prom for juniors. The Ring Dance was less than 8 hours away by that point. As my eyes glared across the computer screen, I knew that it was not going to be a good day. I went through a slew of emotions that included embarrassment, anger, and annoyance that, at the last minute, my date cancelled on me. Not because of a typhoon or a death in the family, but because of the Arctic snow storm that hit the Virginia peninsula the day before.

By Arctic, I mean about a half inch of snow that melted hours after it hit the ground. He went to school about an hour away in Richmond, and for the most part, the weather was pretty similar in his area and in mine. I really wanted to believe his story, and assumed that his school was completely shut down, with folks huddling together to keep warm, making campfires to eat supper. It would have been a bit easier to swallow, had I not left the trailer that my class was in, to see the beautiful sun and wet grass where the "snow" just was. If the sun was any brighter, I might have needed some sunscreen. To add insult to injury, he also claimed his suit jacket was at his mother's and his suit pants were at his dad's. That would make a lot more sense if they didn't live two-and-a-half hours away from each other.

I've never been one to disguise how I feel, so I immediately began to frown and mope around the halls of Bethel High School, like I'd just lost my best friend. In the cafeteria, I watched how everyone else gleamed with excitement about their after school preparation for the dance. I sat there, stone-faced, trying to hold in the tears. Once the bell rang, I walked slowly out of the cafeteria. If I walked any slower, I'd probably have been just standing still. I dreaded hearing my mother's response to my cancelled prom date, because frankly, she wasn't too fond of him either. He hadn't done anything particularly "jerkish" at that point, but she just felt he was too old for me. I began to think she was right. He should have known how important this day was for me. In my mind, he should have bobsledded to Hampton, if need be.

As I left the cafeteria, RJ approached me in the hall. He was his normal, jovial self, which meant even more that I didn't want to hear anything he had to say at that moment.

"Hi Ericka. I heard your date cancelled and I wanted to know if you would go with me."

I can't even remember if I fully looked him in the eye. "I don't know, let me think about it" I responded.

He handed me his number and I believe I crumpled it up and put it in my pocket. Our interaction could not have lasted more than 10 seconds, tops. I kept walking, not sure if he was confused by my response or had totally written me off, but I continued to my car and drove the longest three miles to my house. My mother had already known about my date's cancellation because of the messages he left on the voicemail at home. She knew I would be upset and immediately asked if I was ok.

"Yes. RJ asked me to go but I told him I didn't know" I said nonchalantly. Still, hoping I wouldn't break down into a full-out bawling session with my mother standing there.

"How long ago did he ask you?"

"Just now," I answered. My attitude was just as somber as it had been for the last few hours when I arrived but my mother's eyes immediately sprung open.

"You better call him back right now and tell him you are going," my mother exclaimed. By her tone, I could tell she wasn't too worried about my college stud's cancellation. She wanted to make sure I had a date.

To be honest, I don't even know if my mother knew who RJ was; at that point, I could have cared less. She wanted me to go and enjoy myself and, like my mother suggested, I called RJ and told him I would go. As I dialed, I wasn't nervous, I was a little hopeful that he still wanted to go.

"Hey RJ, I'll go with you."

He sounded as if he had just won the lottery. I believe he did a back-flip within minutes of hanging up the phone.

"I'll call you when I get back from the salon. Bye." This conversation was nearly as quick as the one we had earlier at school. Still no excitement, but at least I wasn't going alone. I headed to the nail and hair salon and began prepping for the dance.

By the time I left the hair salon, I realized that I was a little behind schedule and it was already dark. The dance started at 8 pm and it was past 8 when I returned home. I then realized I was going with someone I had never gone out with before. This could go really good or really bad. Either way, at that point, I was ready for anything. Unfortunately, this was before cell phones, so I had no way of contacting RJ to let him know I was running behind schedule.

By the time I got home, my mother informed me that RJ had already come by looking for me and, to be honest, he looked a bit concerned. I'll admit, I thought it was cute. My mother did not know much about RJ but she knew one thing, he had style. She bragged on his shoes all night, and told me to hurry up and get ready because he was waiting. I got dressed quickly and called RJ to let him know I was ready. He made it to my front door in record time, and he did look very nice, as my mother had described. He had to have been camped out down the street from me. I had no idea how he made it so quickly. He was a gentleman and finally, I was ok with going with him. I was actually looking forward to the night. On the way there, RJ informed me that he had actually gone to various hair salons, looking for me earlier that night. We don't live in a small town and there are dozens of hair salons in the area. I have no idea how he decided which ones to check, but how nice it was for him to search for me, even when he had no idea where to look.

We ended up having a great time at the dance, so while my day started off horribly, it ended on the best note possible. We danced the night away, hung out with friends and laughed all night long. I knew, regardless of my relationship with RJ before the dance, we would be great friends from that point forward. I knew that because of his care and concern for me, at a time when that really was more than necessary.

RJ and I remained friends after the dance, but entering a romantic relationship with him was out of the question for me. For one thing, one of his close friends had a crush on me and we actually dated, for seven whole days. (I know, a whopping week but hey, when you are a teenager, it all counts.) Because of that, I didn't want to be the one who "dated the homie," so I kept RJ in the friend zone. I wasn't aware he had any romantic feelings for me, so it had been a total shock for him to ask me to the Ring Dance. To be honest, I didn't know how he found out about my cancelled college stud so quickly. By the time he asked me that afternoon, I had only known for about half an hour of my date's cancellation. Either way, it turned out fine so I didn't think too much of it.

After the dance, RJ and I hung out a few times. You know how that goes in high school. We grabbed a bite to eat, or we looked at pictures from the Ring Dance, things like that. Actually, RJ turned out to be cooler than I thought. We laughed often and had a good time together. Eventually, we hung out less often; eventually, we started dating other people, just as teenagers do.

RJ's and my friendship continued through high school and into college. We would occasionally catch up on life with each other, but that was the extent of it then. Our colleges were about two hours apart, so we would stay in contact by phone, just a call or text every few months to check in. When I came back home for breaks, we would usually meet up for lunch, and talk about college, who we were dating, etc. Who we were dating was a usual topic for us; I always felt comfort knowing that regardless of what we shared with each other, I wouldn't be judged. That was important to me. I believe being able to have full disclosure is what allows for great relationships.

My first Valentine's Day at college was memorable. At the time, I was dating someone, and despite RJ being aware of this, he sought my sister out and requested my address to send me a Valentine. That year, I had no idea I would get anything from anyone, except for my boyfriend, so when I received a plant, I just assumed it was from him. That was until I read the card. I noticed it was from RJ, and even though I don't quite remember what it said, and it was not overly romantic, I was immediately excited. Not because I wanted to be with him but because he was thinking of me when I assumed he would be chasing skirts at his own school. I called him and thanked him and after a bit of catching up, we hung up. The usual talks for winter/summer breaks occurred and every Valentine's Day after, I would receive a text from him. Despite all the men I dated, RJ was the most consistent.

After college, I moved to Atlanta and RJ stayed local. My first year there I was single, and because of RJ's consistency every Valentine's day, I decided to check in on him for this particular one. We talked for hours and caught up, and just like that, we were back in our routine. During that talk, I did ask him who his Valentine was and he said, "You. Besides my mother, you are the only woman who has been consistent throughout my life." I didn't know what to say. After I thought about it, I realized he was right. We had been in this routine so long that we hadn't realized it had been and was unchanging. Besides my father, RJ was the most consistent man in my life.

About a year or so later, RJ decided he wanted to move to Atlanta so he came to visit and check out the scene. By the scene, I mean the clubs. He arrived around midnight one night, and immediately showered and headed out. We were in our early 20's so that was typical. He made the trip with another childhood friend, and after we caught up that next day, they were on their way back home. A few months later, RJ ended up moving not too far from me, but for some reason, we spoke less. We were both dating other people, and we were engulfed in our own everyday lives. Not even a year later, RJ decided he wanted to head back north; he would be leaving about a month later. While I didn't think it was the best choice, because he hadn't really given Atlanta the time he needed to make it feel like home, it was ultimately his decision to make. Selfishly, I realized he wouldn't be around the corner anymore. Not that we spoke everyday but it was just nice knowing he was there.

Right before he left, my birthday arrived and I invited everyone to a popular stir-fry eatery to celebrate. I was trying to reconcile with my ex at the time, but I was quite annoyed with him at dinner. He had such a lack of enthusiasm with everyone who attended the dinner. He acted as if he didn't want to be there, and that was really putting a damper on my mood. I tried not to let it bother me, so when I saw RJ and our childhood friend arrive, I was elated. They both looked like celebrities! I even teased them that they were "Diddy and Mase." They looked so nice, but I could tell it wasn't for my party. They both bought a drink and informed me they were headed to a local club but wanted to stop by and say hi. RJ did something else bold that that I wasn't expecting. After asking who the guy was (my ex), and turning his nose up a bit, as if saying, he's lame, RJ proudly dropped $50 on the table in front of the hostess when she came by. "This is for my drink and whatever she's getting." We looked at each other and smiled. He left immediately after that. My date, being as uninterested as he was, didn't even care who that guy was that was paying for me, and that annoyed me even more. My sorority sister said, though, "Who is that? I like him." At that moment, I did too.

The time had finally come for RJ to depart for Washington, DC. He came by the night before he was supposed to leave. He didn't stay long, but as he left and we hugged, he looked at me differently from how he had before. He actually lingered a bit. I knew something was different, but I didn't think about it too long. After all, he was moving away.

A few weeks later, I checked on his transition back to D.C. and he told me he had adjusted fine. I was glad to hear that, and just as I was about to head back to work, he texted something I didn't expect. "After I hugged you that day, I really wanted to kiss you but I knew you were with someone and didn't want to disrespect you or your relationship."

If I could have turned white, I would have. My best friend wanted to kiss me? Better yet, the only guy who knew all of my embarrassing moments *still* wanted to kiss me? I didn't know what to say, but at that very moment, something in the dynamic of our relationship changed, because I realized I wanted to kiss him, too.

Needless to say, things were a bit different between us then, and we never brought up the text message again. We were living in two different states and leading two different lives. RJ began pursuing acting more seriously, and when we spoke, he told me about all he wanted to achieve.

About a year or so after he left, my job sent me to Emmitsburg, Maryland for training. I wasn't too thrilled with where I was going, but I was excited to be closer to RJ. My expectations were high for that trip. It would be RJ's and my first meeting since the text confession. While I wasn't sure what it meant for us, I wanted to see him.

Unfortunately, things started off rocky on that trip, starting with my house alarm going off, causing me to leave work early. Thankfully, it was a false alarm. Then, the weather was so bad that my flight was delayed. By the time I boarded the plane, all I wanted to do was sleep. That would have been fine if I had not caught a cold two days prior. My cold was soon exacerbated by the high altitude of the plane ride. I could barely hear out of either ear, along with being super stuffy and congested. I'm sure I roamed the airport like a zombie. When my family called to ensure I made it safely, I yelled, "Huh, what you say?" It was beyond embarrassing. I decided to eat something, knowing chewing might help unclog my ears. It actually worked a little; I was eventually working with "one good ear." To add insult to injury, I missed the bus to the training site and had to wait another hour for the next bus. That hour was coupled with a 45-minute drive to the facility where I would be staying. By the time I arrived to the training site, it was dark and raining and I had no idea where I was going. As the rain began to fall from the sky, so did the tears from my eyes. I cried as I found my dorm for the night and all I wanted to do was sleep.

I woke up thankful that I was safe and warm, but I dreaded going to class because my other ear still had not popped. The next three days were painful, but part of what kept me going was knowing I would see RJ at the week's end. Just as Thursday approached, the pain in my ears had become unbearable, and I decided if I didn't want to be RJ's patient, I should seek some medical attention. The closest urgent care facility seemed a million miles away, and it might as well have been. To get there, I had to travel to another state. By the time I made it to the urgent care, I was exhausted, but excited to finally get some relief.

As the doctor looked into my ear, he said, "Your ear looks likes a 2-year-old's. Why didn't you get here earlier?"

"I was in class," I responded.

"Take these and you should be fine. I'm surprised you aren't rolling on the ground in pain and crying by now," the doc said.

I couldn't cry now. I was only a few short hours away from seeing RJ. I gladly took my prescription to the nearest pharmacist and walked back to the car. I drove back to the room, packed my bags, waved my colleagues *adieu* and began my journey to DC, which was roughly 75-80 miles away. As I made my way onto the interstate, I called RJ to let him know when to expect me. He began to speak, but for a moment, I thought my ear was bothering me again. I thought I heard him say that I had nowhere to park. I hadn't taken a pill yet, so maybe there was some way I heard him incorrectly.

"Excuse me?"

"Yes, they are paving the parking lot here and you won't have anywhere to park?"

I wasn't sure if I should pull over to a rest stop by that time or not. "Are you telling me I have nowhere to park and that is why I shouldn't come? Should I just turn around now?" RJ kept on with the same story, never directly telling me not to come, but implying it. Why didn't he tell me this earlier? I couldn't understand, and I didn't want to at this point. I wanted to click my heels like Dorothy from the "Wizard of Oz" and get home in a blink.

I was stuck. I couldn't go back to where I had been staying because I would have had to explain why I wasn't going to see my "friend," nor could I go to DC, because I couldn't stay with RJ. I did what any girl would do, call her father. Despite my somewhat strained relationship with my dad, I called him and asked him to come get me.

"What happened?" he asked.

"Daddy, I don't want to talk about it. I just need you to come get me."

That day, my father came through in the biggest way. He didn't ask any more questions but came and got me, smiled and took me to his house. He told me he was just glad he could help, and he even made sure I made it to the airport on time the next day. Regardless of what had transpired between my dad and me in the past (I'll address that later), I was "Daddy's little girl" that night. He was my "Knight in Shining Armor," riding to my rescue on his white horse, or Nissan Armada. I have no idea why RJ went through the lengths he did for me not to come that day, and realized I couldn't dwell on it. I didn't speak to him for months after, despite his constant apologies and long-winded explanations.

Once again, RJ and I made up because of the friendship that we built. Our friendship was truly what brought us through many years of disappointments on his end. I now understand why many people say, more than anything else, it's important to be friends first. My history with RJ has taught me many things. First, we all have a choice. Despite the heartbreaks that I dealt with in previous years, I chose RJ, over and over. I have to live with that and understand why I kept making that choice. Second, friendship is key in any relationship, especially a romantic one. There is no way we could have even gotten to the point of being engaged had it not been for our friendship. We all are imperfect humans who will fall short and disappoint the one we love. I believe it's the friendship that will encourage you to forgive and see the heart of that person and not their mistake. Friendship should not be abused as a fall back when you do wrong but strongly believe that coupled with faith, will be a strong bond to break

Chapter 3

Sister, Sis-ta

One of the greatest gifts God has ever given me besides His son Jesus is my twin sister. Don't get me wrong, my parents as well as my other friends and family members are a blessing too but there is something special about having a twin sister. We have bond that is indescribable and when I think about how close we are, I often am brought to tears. We started off in this world together before we even knew what a twin was and have been together every since.

She has been happily married for over the past three years now. Even though the dynamics of our relationship has shifted because her husband is her main confidant (as he should), our bond has never changed. This was demonstrated even more after the engagement ended. I could tell she was hurting just as much as I was because there was absolutely no way she could take the pain from me. She supported me in the best way a sister could and I am forever thankful. I knew her take on this situation would reveal some things to me that I either did not know or did not even realize at the time.

Thank you reader for allowing me to interrupt this story for a moment. My name is Ebony and I'm Ericka's twin sister. My perspective on Ericka's love life will perhaps shed some light on her dating history as well as my perspective on her relationship with RJ.

Aa-aka! That was how I pronounced my twin sister Ericka's name when we were very young. Ebby, a name she still calls me –Ebony-- now, displays the modest, yet sincere way we greet each other. We were literally two peas in a pod.

Growing up, there wasn't anything Ericka would do where I wouldn't be right behind her. Although she was older than me by 5 whole minutes, it seemed more like 5 YEARS. She reached many milestones before me, and that extended throughout our adolescence.

Although we were peers, I looked up to my sister as if she was a much cooler version of myself. She had the rhythm that I always wanted and the confidence I really needed. Ericka didn't have to try to be "cool." People, especially boys, really liked her for not doing much of anything. She was mean and snappy to guys. She would laugh loud, make fun of their clothes….and they LOVED IT! It seems like the meaner she was to them, the more they wanted her. I guess it was a part of her charm.

As we grew and mature, the type of guy that Ericka would date evolved. They were a little rough around the edges, to say the least. Ericka's sass would draw these guys who had a little attitude, but more than enough admiration for her. They were usually nice to her (and to me), but they had a tough façade with everyone else. While she was fun and adventurous as a youth (as in meeting between classes and sneaking phone calls after school), Ericka's taste changed.

At 16, Ericka's boyfriend was something our mother wasn't expecting…..older. He and Ericka met at a summer camp job and fell in infatuation. Ericka was 16 and her boyfriend was 19. We nicknamed him "Ginuwine" for his obvious resemblance. I wondered how this relationship would last. Ericka and I were seen as "the good girls;" we didn't smoke, drink, or do too much of anything rebellious.

However, as a 19-year-old boyfriend in college, he didn't realize this was going to be a relationship rated PG? In the words of Biggie Smalls "If you don't know, now you know." That relationship fizzled after that summer camp job. His obvious lies and disinterest were blatant. The relationship's demise wasn't a surprise or devastation to me. While he was supposed to be Ericka's date to the Ring Dance, he cancelled at the last minute. Luckily, Ericka was able to get another date within a few hours...RJ.

Sidenote Readers: "Ginuwine's" excuse for not being able to attend the Ring Dance was that the jacket to his suit was in one city and the pants were in another☐ Very original.....

RJ attended middle school and high school with us; he was quiet, but was a very nice person to all he encountered. A romantic relationship with Ericka would be the last thing I would have expected for them. They'd always had a cordial relationship, but nothing out of the ordinary.

Ericka was really in a jam with the Ring Dance being a few hours away, and not having a date at the last minute. RJ stepped in as a great friend, in her time of need. He bought a matching suit to compliment what Ericka was going to wear. He even went looking for Ericka in weird, local, hair salons, when we were running late to the dance. They took great pictures together.....a picture that would come up again 10 years later.

As high school and college came upon us, Ericka dated several other guys who would be mainstays. Ericka's first college beau would be around for several years. She met him right before we graduated high school. He was also from our hometown, but he was very different from the guys she had dated in the past. He was much shorter than the rest (about 5'8") and he was a real intellectual. He was also very honest with Ericka. He was not afraid to tell Ericka exactly how he felt, but more than anything, he adored her. He was wide open. The way he would look at her, the way he would talk about her, the way he wanted to connect with her, was unlike any other beau she'd had before. While it was sweet and affectionate, it wouldn't last. We were 21. Was it supposed to? Well, maybe, but it didn't that time.

They grew apart and Ericka met another beau, a tall African man who was a gentle giant of sorts. He was very protective of Ericka and I. He would give us pizza money for dinner. I think I remember him tucking me into my dorm room bed once....he was that kind of guy. Like the first college beau, he adored Ericka, as well, and he wasn't afraid to let us know it! He was in a fraternity, and during his frat's probate, he made a whole dedication to her and to our sorority. It was so unexpected, but so genuine. I knew he would be THE ONE. Ericka, the beau, and I moved to Atlanta after graduation and I knew it was a matter of time before all of us would be a family (Funny how I included me in there too.).

Once we moved to Atlanta, though, he became a different person. I remember him getting upset at Ericka for not knowing which country he was from in Africa. Ericka did something then, that I had never seen her do. She internalized someone else's perception of her. She seemed to be shaken by his words. She seemed unsure of herself, and I didn't like it. It appeared that she was trying to prove her worth with each encounter, each visit. I was not used to seeing my sister like that, and I was hoping that relationship would end. After a year or so of back-and-forth, and semi-relationships, she ended it. I think the last straw was her spending Valentine's Day by herself....Thank goodness the tall African man was gone; not thank goodness Ericka was spending that day alone.

From that point on, Ericka had different relationships here and there. Some were semi-serious; some were laughable moments. That was until she met a man at the Glen Hotel. That relationship would last a little over a year, and it would leave her broken. She loved him and loved him hard. He loved her the same way. They appeared to enjoy each other and embrace each other's families. He and I also became close. He helped me move into my new home, days before my own wedding. I thought Ericka had found THE ONE.

Just days after the New Year, 2012, the bomb dropped. When I thought Ericka would be getting engaged to him, he was breaking up with her! When she told me, I thought she was lying, like she was just waiting to surprise me with her new engagement ring. Instead, she surprised me with tears and heartache.

It seems like it came out of nowhere, and she was to blame, at least according to him. He blamed their whole demise on one incident that had taken place 8 or 9 months before. I wasn't buying it.....In retrospect he did her a favor but it hurt so bad to see Ericka so sad. I felt helpless. I vowed to myself that I would never see her that way again.

Fast forward 8 months later. RJ stepped back into the picture. My sister seemed happier than she had been in a long time. They had a connection that all could see. It appeared that when they saw each other they picked up where things had left off. They threw a great cookout and really appeared to be heading in the right direction. They cooked, they danced, and simply loved being around each other that night. I knew he may have been a bit inebriated, but later that evening, he took me into my sister's room and told me he was going to ask my sister to marry him.

I was so excited.....I didn't know what to do. I told him I would help him every step of the way. I had my ring finger sized and looked at pictures of rings he emailed to me. Most important (to me anyway), was that he was also going to move to Atlanta. It didn't get any better than that. I was sold! Next, was keeping it a secret, and I did a pretty good job with that. Once he proposed, and she accepted, I was so happy for her, for them, and I was happy to have been a part of their decision.....until I regretted helping at all.

I never thought that I would have to support my sister on that cold, January, Thursday night. I remember feeling relieved in one way; my sister wouldn't have to move across the country. She could see and support my new family, and I could support hers, but I just couldn't imagine my husband and me not getting married. I couldn't imagine that he would ask me to be his wife, but then not marry me. I couldn't imagine having to be the one to initiate the end of our engagement, the end of our life together. I would never want my sister to experience that.

I also didn't know what to do to comfort her. I didn't know what to say or do. I remember telling her I would drive over and comfort her.....until she told me "Scandal" was on.…

Now fast forward to December 13, 2014. Nearly two years after the engagement ended, my sister is about to embark on her first speaking engagement at a Women's Conference entitled, "I Chose to Live." As my sister walks to the podium, all eyes are on her. She starts with a prayer. My eyes well up with emotion and admiration that everything she has been through has bought her to this point. More than anything, I saw how this book will be a blessing to others.

The women all looked eagerly at Ericka, maybe because of her beauty. I think it was more because of her message.

Chapter 4

Groundhog Day

It has been two month since the engagement has been called off and I'm hoping today will be that day where no one asks me about it. I realize that at this point, most people don't know, but I was tired of not only having to explain myself, but also of the look most people gave me after my explanation. It was a mix of sorrow and confusion about what happened and how many questions they could ask me.

On one day in particular, I was starting to feel more like my old self and was looking forward to going to work and interacting with my co-workers. Lately, I had been saying hi and bye so quickly, one would think I was auditioning for the Olympic track team. As I sat at my computer that day, the IT guy from the first floor tapped me from behind. He said, "Congratulations!" I was a little confused, but since he was grinning from ear to ear, all I could think of to say was, "Thank you." He kept smiling, so I finally asked "What are you referring to?" I almost forgot that it had only been a few months prior that I was engaged. "Your engagement. I know I'm late. I saw it on Facebook a while ago." I smiled and said "Oh." I looked at the expression on his face a little longer. I wasn't sure what to say or if I should say anything. After contemplating for a few seconds, I decided I just couldn't do it. I couldn't lie.

"Well, actually, there is not going to be a wedding." I point at my ring finger, which was currently bare. His face dropped. He looked confused and a little embarrassed. "I'm so sorry. Wow. I guess I'm really late." We both laughed. His next few words were very short. I could tell he was uncomfortable. I felt like I had been in a time when I thought I would be the one who needed a great deal of comfort (and at times I did). Oddly enough, it had been freeing to be able to help others, especially at a time when I felt I needed help the most.

I think Joel Osteen said it best in his book, *From your Best Life Now*. *"If you believe for your child to find God, go help somebody else's child to develop a relationship with God. If you're struggling financially, go out and help somebody who has less than you have ... [Y]ou want to reap financial blessings, you must sow financial seeds in the lives of others ... If you want to see healing and restoration come to your life, go out and help somebody else get well"* (pp. 224, 250-51).

I'll admit, that all sounded good in theory, but I wasn't sure I wanted to practice it, not realizing I was doing it more than I thought. At a time when I was hurting, I did not always feel like helping others, or making others feel at ease. At times, though, it helped me get through. I could focus on someone else instead of myself. That moment with the IT guy helped me realize my strength in a time of weakness.

Sometimes, when you feel you can't go on, you have to look inside of yourself and find that strength and the courage to move forward. At a time in your life when you feel as if your days run together and you have to answer the same questions over and over, you have to *be* the difference in that day. You have to have a different attitude. Had I rolled my eyes at that question, or shut down because I felt that he was taking me to a place that I was tired of being (heartache), it could have ruined the rest of a day that had begun as a great day. I wasn't going to let a question take away the peace I had. Feeling like you can help someone, despite your situation, is a true testimony to the goodness of God and what He can do in your life.

After that euphoric moment, I realized how blessed I was. I drove home, ready to cook dinner for my girlfriends, and I received another phone call. This time, from a company that stated that RJ and I had won a free vacation somewhere, because of registering for something that we likely didn't really register for at all. My best friend was over, and I know she was eavesdropping, so I wasn't sure how to respond. Ultimately, I had to tell them I was no longer marrying RJ and, of course, the person on the other end of the phone was apologetic. That was the second awkward moment of the day. My best friend asked, "Who was that?" I then had to go into who called and why, thus creating another uncomfortable moment.

I looked up at my ceilings for cameras. I wondered if I was being punked? Were random people staggered throughout my day just to aggravate me? From my coworker, whom I saw every blue moon, to a random telemarketer, being punked was my only logical explanation. Remember all that peace I just referenced in the first paragraph? It was nearly an afterthought at that point.

It's crazy how a few moments can ruin your mood, just like that. One question a day was okay for me, but to be confronted two times in less than 4 hours? Come on! I know those of you who have experienced this understand what I'm saying. It only takes a second to go from glee to gloom. I think this experience has really shown me what joy really means. I read something on one of my friend's Twitter pages that stated how one would rather have joy than happiness, because happiness is only experienced when you are in that state. Joy is experienced despite your circumstances and is a choice. That really put things in perspective for me and made me appreciate the joy God has given me to tap into. Sometimes you may not tap; you have to knock hard for that joy. We all have it, we just have to know how and when to access it. For me, when I started feeling discouraged, sad or just plain angry about what had happened to me, I remembered all of the good things in my life such as my health, my family and how blessed I was to have supportive people around me. What more could I ask for? I had so much to be thankful for.

A friend of mine had recently gone into the hospital after a freak accident and was fighting for his life. I went to the hospital to visit him and was shocked by what I saw. He was unrecognizable. At that moment, I knew that things could always be worse. Take out a sheet of paper or use your phone or tablet. Write out all you have to be thankful for. There is nothing too big or too small. During times when you feel you need a pick-me-up, consult that list. Keep it handy so you can find it quickly. Sometimes, you just have to see your blessings written out to appreciate them.

Now before you go and find my ex and tie him to a tree, let me make a few things clear. He's not a bad person. He didn't cheat, abuse me or any other "ratchet" things that are way too common in our society. I did feel that he lied though. Not about another women or another man. He lied about wanting to be a husband, about wanting to spend the rest of his life with me.

The proposal should have gone more like: "I want to spend the rest of my life with you as long as my career is first." I know it sounds selfish. At least to me it is. But to his defense, I don't think he thought that far. It's easy to fall into the fairy-tale, that all you need is love to be happy. Everything will work itself out. It's catchy. It's romantic. It makes you feel warm inside. But as many of you know, it takes a lot more than love to have a happy and successful relationship. Love may be the basis, but you need to have trust, similar views on life, and on parenting; you have to have an agreement on where to raise your family, etc. I think that is something that both of us took for granted. We always knew we loved each other, but we would soon realize that we needed so much more, to have the life that we so desired.

I must reiterate, RJ is not a monster. If he was, I wouldn't have been his friend for so many years and even accepted his marriage proposal. I'm no monster lover. When a relationship goes sour, we tend to only think of the negative things and how bad a person he/she was. We must remember that, if we did that, what would that make us? I know that while he was not a monster, he was someone who was very focused on his career. He moved away from his family and across the country to pursue his dream. I admired that about him. I know that it wasn't an easy decision to make, but it was necessary for growth in his career.

It's crazy that the thing I admired most about him would be the thing that would tear us apart. His desire to become the best actor cost him a lot more than missing his friends and family. It cost him me. I don't know if he realized that before I told him the night we broke up. When I reiterated that point, the only thing he could say was....nothing.

After over ten years of friendship, nearly four months of being engaged, and years of me forgiving him for always choosing his feelings over mine, this man had nothing to say. No fight, no begging. I assumed he must really be talking but he must have accidently pressed the "mute" button on his end. To my dismay, the phone was working fine. It was my ears that couldn't comprehend what was happening. Not only was I shocked he had nothing to say, but now I was angry. To be honest, I should not have been. This was usually the case. RJ and I didn't have drag out screaming matches. Most huge disagreements we had ended with me asking him a question and RJ not responding; me getting irritated from his lack of response and the phone call ending. It was pretty consistent over the years, so how foolish of me to think this would be different.

If I learned nothing else, I should have taken away that when people show you who they are, believe them, the first time. But hey, I wouldn't be where I am today without some of the lessons that I have learned. A friend once told me that God will continue to teach you a lesson until you learn it. I'm confident that, while this is a lesson that took me some time to learn, I finally can say I passed.

What lessons has God been trying to teach you? When I say, "try," here, it's not because God can't figure out a way to get through to you, it's because you haven't been able to grasp what He has been trying to say. This not only applies to romantic relationships, but also to family, co-workers, this list could go on for days. At one time, I thought I made the biggest mistake ever by not marrying RJ and it would take me years to overcome it. It took me 28 years to get engaged, so how many years would it take me to be engaged to someone else and actually married? These thoughts consumed me for some time. I had to realize, God doesn't punish us the way society does. When we make a mistake and repent, He forgives us immediately and it's erased. As long as we are breathing, we can rectify our wrongs. Every day I wake up is a day to start over, start new. When I get up every morning, one of the first things I say, or think, or mumble is thank you God. I used to only think I was thanking Him because I woke up that morning. I was safe, sound, healthy and had a job to go to. As I grow spiritually, I realize that the fact I have another day, means I have another day to start over, to right my wrongs, and to fix things. This not only goes for the person that has been hurt, but for the person who may be hurting others. It's just as easy to stay in a slump because we are a heartbreaker, as it is to be heartbroken.

In the relationship I was in after RJ, he was notorious for being a heartbreaker. He cheated and lied to numerous women and was even married and divorced a few years prior to meeting me. Our conversations revealed to me that he carried that shame just like I did, despite us being on opposite sides of the relationship. I would remind him, when he came to God and asked for forgiveness, he was forgiven. I expressed that God forgiving him and him forgiving himself were two different things.

I truly believe that one reason God sent me the man I dated after my relationship with RJ was so that I would actually get to see what RJ was feeling. Some of the things this man said were just a bit too eerie. Statements such as, "I think my ex will hate me forever. People will always look at me as a monster because of what I did. I don't know how I could forgive myself."

Guilt is a tool used by the Devil to keep us trapped and captive in our thoughts. We have to be cognizant of our thoughts and, when we feel our minds shift; we have to get back to the place of peace. I could sense they were things that RJ would say and feel. It's hard to describe, or even explain, but it was like God was trying to show me that despite the break up being his idea, he was hurting just as much, or even more, than I was. Knowing that gave me some solace. Nobody wants to feel like they are hurting alone. Despite the hurt he caused, I don't believe RJ ever intended to hurt me, someone that he truly loved.

In one of my last conversation with RJ through texting, as we closed out our bank account for the wedding, he said something that was hard for me to read for a while. "I will always love you." I woke up to that text and, at the time, all I could do was cry. I wanted to believe that, but it was hard. How could someone who will always love me, hurt me to this degree? Deep down, I knew it was true, but it wasn't a truth I was ready to face. At least, not then.

Another day may mean more questions from those around you, wondering what happened, but it doesn't mean that your life will be stuck where you are. Nearly eight months after our engagement was called off, I had another co-worker ask when I was getting married. This time, instead of it being awkward, I smiled and said, "Where have you been? It's been over for a while." I know he was shocked, but just knowing I could smile about the break-up has given me the strength and faith of knowing that another day, when I will actually get married is on the horizon.

God can take you to heights that you never knew and never imagined. I didn't believe that in even eight months, I would be smiling instead of frowning. I would hear of engagements and not think about the pain that I endured, but I would reminisce about the joy I know that bride to be is feeling. I know it may sound cheesy and corny, but it excites me to know that, every day God wakes me, I'm getting closer to my dream.

Get excited, you never know what your "another day" has in store for you.

Chapter 5

Purge

I always say that when a break up occurs with someone I'm dating, they think I've moved to another continent because they will probably never see or hear from me again. It's not that I go into hiding or try to avoid places where I think I may run into them. I promise! It has just been the case that I've dated a few guys in the city where I live, but have not run into them at stores, movies, etc. I'm blessed that I have never had one of those awkward exchanges where you see them with someone else or vice versa. Breakups are hard enough.

In conjunction with never seeing them, I make the choice to delete their name from my phone, social media, as well as put away all memorabilia that would make me think of them. Harsh, I know. Why do all of that, you ask? My experiences have shown me that it's easier to move on, once that person has been removed from your life in all aspects. Try it. The first few days are the hardest but there will come a time when you will start to feel normal…when you won't be tempted to check your phone all the time to see if you missed a call. You won't be inclined to stalk their Facebook, Instagram or Twitter page for updates. Out of sight, out of mind is something I live by; for me, it has worked pretty well.

Breaking off an engagement was no exception. In fact, those rules were even stricter because of the severity of the situation. After I got off the phone with RJ, and placed the ring into its original box, I strategically took our pictures off of my dresser. When I came home, after spending some time at my sister's and brother-in law's home, I returned to my room, armed with a trash bag. My sister had come back with me, too. I began to dump almost everything RJ had ever given me, with my sister rooting me on. When I say rooting me on, I don't mean yelling or screaming at me to put a knife to his stuff or stomp on some of the more fragile items. It was silent. She didn't say a word while I grabbed things from the shelf and placed them in the dark trash bag. She was there in the event I couldn't handle it and THAT made all the difference. Every picture was trash. I gathered all of my wedding materials and dumped them too.

Now when it came to the gifts, I was a little more liberal. The Michael Kors bag? I definitely still carry it, but I didn't start doing that immediately after. I'm no fool. RJ had just given it to me a few weeks prior, so I didn't have a great deal of time to attach the gift to him. The bracelets for Christmas? I still wear them. After a breakup, a few people told me I should give or throw away any reminders of that person. I considered it, but I knew I liked both items and wouldn't be able to part as easily with them. They were almost like parting gifts, for everything I had been through.

Determining what to throw away is totally up to you. Just because you decide to keep a few things doesn't mean you aren't over it. How you choose to look at the items do. If I carry the purse just to have a piece of him left with me then, yes, the bag should go. I felt mature enough to keep it; sometimes, I forget he gave it to me and that lets me know that it was okay to keep it.

Ericka McCracken

I thought that I would be a bit more emotional, as I discarded our memories in a trash bag, but it was actually freeing. Having my sister with me gave me assurance that I was not alone. I think it's best for anyone going through an experience like mine to have only one person present, two max, for emotional support. Doing the clearing of items and memories by yourself could cause you to linger longer than you should.... holding mementos and cradling them like newborns. The experience of clearing is hard enough, so I believe the process should be as quick as possible. The sooner the things are out of your home, the easier it will be to move on. That's not to say that you may not envision those items there, despite them being physically and materially gone. With time, you will replace them with new items and memories. In my case, I replaced a photo album of us with a piggy bank and actually forget, sometimes, that all of those reminders of our love had ever been there.

The sooner, the better, is a good rule of thumb to follow. There will be so many reminders that you can't throw away, but for the ones you can get rid of, you must. Your favorite song, his favorite show, are just two of countless numbers of other things you can't just ball up and

91

throw in the dumpster. I have come to realize that purging is more than just taking reminders of that relationship out of your life. It's about truly getting out your emotions, thoughts, and feelings, especially negative ones, to make room for all the good that is about to come into your life.

I purged my emotions to a counselor, someone who had no idea of my track record, or what I had just endured. I wanted to hear an honest opinion and had an idea of where to go. I waited about two months or so after the engagement was over before starting counseling. I wanted to eliminate as much baggage as I could, so I would not take it into my next relationship. I met with a counselor for just a few sessions and, immediately, I knew this was not the counselor for me. She seemed gentle with her approach but she was very judgmental. For example, I told her my parents separated for over five years before they divorced. She had the absolute nerve to ask what took them so long to finalize it, because divorces aren't that expensive. She was completely out of touch. My mother was raising two teenagers on her own, with no support from my father at the time, and that counselor had the nerve to ask what took so long. She almost got a "girl bye" from me after that, but

I decided to stay. After my initial frustrations with her wore off, I noticed she did have insight on *some* things.

The counselor discussed the way I romanticized relationships, and how I pretty much took men for face value. I did not allow them to prove themselves. Whatever a man said to me, in regards to our relationship and what his plans were for me, I believed it. I assumed that if he said it, it must be true. Who would lie to me? Right. Foolish huh? That revelation, while startling, was something I knew I would have to work on in the future. Despite my disconnection with this counselor, I knew there was something from her sessions that would help me in my quest for healing.

If you have been to counseling before, don't hesitate to go back. If you've never been, consider it. It was one of the best decisions I have ever made. Also, remember that if you don't like the counselor that you have, don't be afraid to ask for another. There's nothing wrong with interviewing counselors until you get the one from whom you will benefit most. After all, you are paying for it. You might as well get what you need. I believe speaking to someone who is impartial, and has no history of your past, outside what you tell them, will help you immensely. Talking to a friend may help for a moment, but it's rare that friends can give you the best advice that may hurt, but is needed during this period. Our friends have our best interest at heart, and they will protect us at all costs, even to our detriment at times. Talking to a third party can help you see things that others who are involved with you might miss.

For me, counseling helped illuminate a vulnerable side that I was too scared to show to my friends. I was fearful that they would view me as weak. As ironic as that sounds, that was a huge fear of mine. I've always prided myself on being the strong one in the group, so to show that level of helplessness was something I wasn't ready for at that time. I began to examine my rawest feelings and asked myself many questions.

What thoughts dominate your head? Thoughts that you will never love again? Or that you will never find someone who understands you like him? I realized that, in order for me to find joy and really get to the other side of my emotions, I had to purge those thoughts immediately and find new ones to occupy my mind. If those thoughts tend to roam rampant, it's vital that you change your thought processes. Whether it's your favorite Bible verse or saying, make sure there is something to combat the negative thoughts you are ridding yourself of.

One of my favorite verses is Philippians 4:7, "And the peace of God, which surpasses all understanding, will guard your hearts and your minds in Christ Jesus." That verse brings me peace every time I think about it. Whatever verse or quote you choose, commit it to memory so you can bring it to the forefront of your mind when necessary. Trust me; you will need it more than you think. Pick a verse that you can commit to memory that gives you peace every time you read it or say it to yourself.

I like to think of it as a way of speaking to your mountains. One mountain may be doubts about love and your future. The verse that you choose will help you break down that mountain and see past it. One of your mountains can be so large that you cannot even begin to imagine what's on the other side of it. It could be dark on the other side, but I always believe it's bright and even prettier than I could have ever imagined. One of my Facebook friends, Melvin Davis, put it best when he stated, *"Believe you can experience someone better than the person you once longed for or were with. Believing that there isn't someone else out there better is a lie. Qualities of brains and beauty, emotional and spiritual maturity, confidence and ambition, can be found anywhere in this world. The person you once had or desired isn't the only one on this planet who can move your heart. Speak the love of your life into existence, and believe."*

I believe wholeheartedly that God had something better in store for me and that's why it didn't work out. In hindsight, I know He does, and while it was hard to go through the storm, the sun on the other side has been awesome.

I would be remiss to say that along with purging things and emotions, I had to purge my tears. They needed to be released. For the longest, I thought crying was for babies and weak women. No one ever told me that; my mother didn't instill that in me with her words. I just put two and two together and figured because I never saw my mom cry, and she was the strongest woman I knew, I shouldn't cry either. During my parent's separation, she was always standing. In my adolescent eyes, it never fazed her. I didn't see her down but, oddly enough, I saw her happier. She had a new zest about life. She was happy to come home from work and spend time with her girls. We soon became the Three Musketeers. My mother, sister, and I would shop together, go to the movies, and spend most of the quality time away from work and school with each other. When we faced adversities, we did so together. I remember when my mother's alternator wasn't working well and her car would not start up at times. My mother and sister would walk to work to pick me up at 10:00pm. My mother usually went to bed around 7:30pm. As tired as she was from working 12-16 hour days, she made sure her baby made it home safely. I saw my mother's strength, not her emotions. As I grew into a woman, I realized just how my mother was feeling. During break ups, I put on the brave face for my mother. I told her I was okay so she wouldn't worry, despite crying myself to sleep some nights, and having my weight fluctuate from lack of an appetite. The same brave face my mother had, I inherited. I may have overdosed on the "happy pill" after a break up, but I realize it's not as healthy as everyone thinks.

Emotion, whether good or bad, is healthy as long as it is expressed appropriately. Purge those tears after your relationship ends. When someone asks how you are, tell them if you are hurting or if you aren't having the best day. It's ok. I'm learning that, and usually when I talk about it, I feel better. Like I stated earlier, I don't want people to think that I don't feel or don't hurt. I just choose to channel it differently. I believe it's important for others to see the ugly just as well as the beautiful.

Chapter 6

The Ring

Now, this can be touchy. Depending on the circumstances, a woman may think she is entitled to keep THE RING! I'm not here to say, either way, what you should do; it is an individual and personal choice. I recall a few years ago, right before my trip to California, I was watching one of those TV court shows. This case involved a man suing his ex-fiancé over the engagement ring he gave her. I remember watching so attentively, thankful that it wasn't me on that stand.

I honestly felt bad for the defendant. I could see she was clearly still shaken up over the break-up. After both sides pled their cases, the judge's verdict was…she had to give the ring back.

The man was super excited, and you could tell by looking at him that he knew exactly what he was going to do with the money he would get from the ring. On the other hand, the woman looked speechless and didn't know what to do. You could tell that she was stunned the verdict had not been in her favor. She stated she was in counseling, but looked as if she needed her counselor that very minute. As eerie as it must have been, it was *her* reality at that moment. Little did I know, weeks later, I would be faced with the same decision.

In my case, I knew that the ring would be going back immediately. I had no desire for it, nor was there a place I would have liked to store it. I mean sure, I could have thrown it in a box, but for what? To collect dust or to find unexpectedly, once I became engaged to a man I was sure to marry. I thought about it and took a pass. Our engagement ended on a Thursday, and by Monday, I had the ring boxed up. I nearly met the postal workers at the post office when they opened for business. I knew, besides returning the wedding dress, this would further seal the end of this chapter of my life. As I wrote the address on the box, I wondered what RJ would do when he received it.

Would he open it? Stare at it and cry, like I had a few days prior? Or, stuff it in the back of his closet, because it was too hard to look at?

Whatever he did, I knew the ring had no room in my house anymore, or in my life. I chose to return the ring simply because it wasn't mine. I thought of pawning it to pay off the wedding dress I couldn't return, but I figured I wouldn't get much back anyways. At the end of the day, it was his now and I was glad to rid myself of it. I wasn't emotional because I knew that, one day, I would have a ring that would never leave my finger and I couldn't get that ring, as long as this ring was in my possession.

Circumstances are different, so for whatever reason, your decision may be different from mine. My decision was neither right nor wrong; it was MINE. That was what worked for me, and may work for one of you reading this. Just know that if vengeance is your reason for keeping the ring, it won't make you any happier. It will just be a constant reminder of what could have been.

I spoke to a friend recently, who had kept all of her wedding memorabilia in a box, and toted it from location to location with her when she moved. She didn't know what to do with it; she thought maybe she and her ex might reconcile one day.

I suggested she burn that box and watch it go up in flames. I know, harsh. I probably said that to her because I knew all the drama she went through with her ex and couldn't understand why she would want to keep those memories. I should have taken my own advice. She had to make the best decision for her, regardless of what I had done, had said, or had believed.

While I had a few items that I could do without, I didn't have picture albums or invitations like I would have had from an actual wedding. I couldn't imagine how hard it would be to part with all of that. On the other hand, I have another friend whose wedding I attended, and she, too, still had her items. Her divorce was final after only one year of marriage. While she didn't burn the items like I suggested with my other friend, she had moved on completely from that incident, and because of a move, she hadn't gotten around to going through everything. After all, her wedding and everything around that day had been a part of her life that dozens of friends and families had witnessed. She wasn't bitter, but she wasn't sure exactly what to do with everything. In time, I know both of my friends will do what's best for them and I'll support them all the way...I promise!

Now, don't get me wrong, I've been on the answering end of the ring dilemma, too. People asked me what I did with the ring, and I thought then, and still think, that question is rather invasive. I felt like they might as well have asked for my Social Security Number.

I know it's a stretch but after all I went through, I did not want to hear remarks like, "I would have done so and so and so." Whether to just be nosy, or because they thought it was nice of me to have returned it, it was none of their business. Nevertheless, it amazed me how men's faces lit up when I said I returned the ring. On the other hand, women's faces scowled as soon as the "sent it back" words left my lips.

If you feel like answering, by all means, do so. If not, I think it may be better to answer with "It's personal." I do feel that a line has to be drawn somewhere. With all the emotions, questions to deal with, and the explaining one must do in the break-up predicament, answering the ring question can make you feel like there is a right answer. There isn't. Whether you decide to keep the ring, or not, just make sure it's your decision and not something you feel you should do. Ultimately, you are the one who will have live with it.

I doubted RJ would try to re-gift the ring, or that he could even get half of what he paid for it. To be honest, if he did, it's no longer my concern. I can only hope the next time he gets on one knee, it will be in front of the person he will undoubtedly spend the rest of his life with.

What did you do with your ring? Do you feel at peace about it? I sometimes wonder what ever happened to that woman I saw on court TV that day. I hope she is doing better and has not only emotionally let go of losing the ring, but she has emotionally let go of losing her fiancé, as well. It almost seemed as if that was the last piece of him that she had left, and she was holding on to it for dear life. I won't forget the pain I saw in her eyes, or the expression on her face when the verdict was read. While society looks at the monetary value of engagement and wedding rings, the receiver of those rings sees much more. The commitment, the promise, and the love it was given in. I think that is why it wasn't even a second thought for me to part with it. I knew that commitment was broken, the promise wouldn't be kept, and the love would soon dissipate.

I know this sounds super sad and, quite frankly blunt, but I choose to look at it as a new beginning. While these things happen, new commitments, new promises, and new loves happen for people every day. I knew it would be a matter of time before new beginnings would come my way again.

One take-away from this situation has less to do with the ring, and more to do with everything else about the wedding. We didn't get extremely far in the planning process, but I had already purchased a dress; we had secured a venue; and we were about to secure a caterer. I had the task of canceling all the plans that were made. No one should have to bear the brunt of having to make all of those phone calls by themselves. RJ would have helped, if I had asked, but like Superwoman, I felt like I didn't need him and could do it all by myself. Boy was I wrong! I should have given him at least one call to cancel one thing.

It may almost seem easier to handle matters ourselves, because let's face it, men tend not to be as thorough as we would like them to be, and as we are, ourselves. Even during the wedding planning, I chose to make the majority of the decisions, and included him just because I knew I would get it done. I am a planner at my current day job, so it just came naturally. I knew what I wanted, and I didn't have full confidence that he would complete it in the manner that I saw fit.

I know, a typical woman huh?

That's something I'm working on for future relationships, as well. No one will probably ever do things just the way I do, except for my twin, and that's just because of our bond and the fact that we see most things the same way. I have to learn to trust more, and not just about matters of the opposite sex in a relationship, but with mundane things in a relationship, and in a marriage one day. Even with the cancellation process, I just knew that I would get things done, and quickly, so I decided to spearhead everything. It did get done, but tearing up and nearly breaking down after every call could have been avoided.

If you are in this boat right now, trust your ex, or if you don't think you can, let someone close to you help in these matters. I began to resent RJ after everything was completed, thinking he didn't bother to lift a finger, but could I really blame him? I didn't ask for his help, and just like in the wedding planning process, I handled most of everything. Why would this be any different? Trust is so important and will help you more than you could ever think.

Telling your family and friends is another task you don't have to handle alone. When I had to call my parents and tell them the wedding was off, and the relationship was over, my sister was right by my side, holding my hand as I held back the tears. Those were the toughest conversations I had ever had with them, but knowing I had someone there to comfort me made it a little easier. There are some conversations that will have to be had, so before the calls, make sure you pray and have someone there to rub your back or hold your hand along the way. It may seem juvenile, but trust me, you *will* need someone. Luckily for me, my parents asked few questions and really supported my decision, and were there to help.

They both are out of state, so it was hard for them to come and comfort me physically, but I'm thankful that they supported me in my time of need. Now, I know that no two parents are just alike, so if you have parents who may be a bit more intuitive, it is especially important for you to have that friend there by your side. They could be able to take over the conversation (in a respectful way), if it becomes too much for you to bear, and they could also ensure your loved ones that you are in good hands. That's typically what the parents are most concerned about.

My sister was really good about sending emails and texts to friends about the broken engagement, so I wouldn't have to field such calls, emails, texts, tweets, etc. I trusted her and knew that she would give the information that I wanted released about the matter. Whoever your closest confidant is, entrust him or her with the task of fielding queries from friends and families about the relationship. Just as a maid of honor would serve the bride at a wedding, you will need that person to be of service to you during your break-up and its aftermath. Trust me, your confidant and friend will be more helpful than you can imagine.

Chapter 7

Alone vs. Lonely

Both words have quite a few of the same letters, don't they? But they have very different meanings. After any break up, the first days, weeks, and even months will be difficult, especially after breaking off an engagement. Once you decide you are getting married, you start planning a life in your mind. Having to re-think, or erase those thoughts, is even more overwhelming.

As a believer, I knew I had to give it to God. I had to allow Him to figure it out, because at times, it was too much of a burden to bear. I had to consistently remind myself that He knew what was best and already had it figured out for me. When the thoughts became too heavy for me, I would recall Jeremiah 29:11, "God has plans for me, to prosper and not to harm me. Plans for a future." That in itself was enough to put my mind at ease on many of those first, difficult days.

As I said before, it's vital for you pick a scripture or two to memorize when you get those feelings, because they are sure to hit you when you least expect it.... watching a movie.... walking down the street as a couple passes you..... while you're watching TV...... or on social media sites. You wouldn't bring a knife to a gunfight, so it's equally important to arm yourself with God's word.

Now that you have your protection (the Word), it's important to know what else you may be up against. In addition to those unpleasant lies, you also will be up against the feelings of loneliness.

One way to look at "alone" and "lonely," is that one is a state, and the other is a feeling. The definition of, alone, from the Merriam Webster dictionary is, "separated from others or exclusive of anyone or anything else." Now while we may have times where we are physically by ourselves, we must have comfort knowing God is with us and He is our present help (Psalm 46:1). That gave me comfort, especially after going back to my house after a week at my sister and brother-in-law's home.

I walked into an ice-cold house (it was winter) and felt like it was similar to how my life was at that time. However, once I walked up stairs, clicked on the heat, and began to unpack and clean, I began to feel warm. I then turned on the stove to cook, and then clicked on the TV. By the time I feel asleep, it all felt normal, I was back in my routine. Normalcy met me again.

You see, the only way to start to feel like yourself again is to do the things you would normally do. Before you know it, you are back in your routine, like you haven't skipped a beat. Now, if your ex was the one who washed the dishes while you cooked or vice versa, and helped you with those routine things, it will be an adjustment, but that's expected. Just keep at it and know that those feelings will pass.

To the contrary, the feeling of loneliness requires more time and energy to combat. I have felt lonely in a room full of people, so it's not so much the physical as it is the emotional being. You could just try to replace your ex with someone to try to avoid that feeling of loneliness, but you will eventually have to face it. You are essentially putting a Band-Aid on a bullet wound. Temporarily, you may feel better, but those emotions, if not addressed, will fester and most likely come out in an unlikely, unproductive way.

In my case, RJ lived across the country so I was used to him not being there on a daily basis. I knew that, soon, we would be starting our life together, so it would be a temporary circumstance. Once things ended, I felt, at times, that this loneliness, physically and emotionally, would last forever. Once again, the Deceiver wanted me to feel that my temporary unhappiness would be a long-term rut I would never get out off. I knew that I had to do something, and quick. I learned the feeling of loneliness could become so overwhelming that it could make you feel like your situation is permanent and won't change.

During this time, it's important to keep occupied. I'm sure you've heard the saying: Idle time is the Devil's playground. It's not only true for children, it's true for adults, too. You don't want to feel so alone you call up an ex just for comfort and companionship. It may feel good momentarily, but the reason you broke up in the first place will soon resurface and you will be back at square one. Trust me, I've done this too many times and the results have always been the same. You wouldn't buy food from a place that smelled good but didn't pass the state health test? Looks and emotions can be deceiving which is why they shouldn't lead us.

One of the reasons I dread having to start over in relationships is because of the "dry period" that I have typically gone through when one relationship has ended. After my college boyfriend and I broke up, I didn't have another boyfriend for nearly four years. You heard it right, four years. I didn't want to face that ugly truth of possibly having to wait another four years to be in a relationship. When I was 22, it seemed bad, but at 29, I felt like my clock was ticking.

Don't get me wrong, I dated guys in between those years, but it took that long for me to be in a committed relationship with someone. Looking back, I realize I didn't know what I really wanted. I had this ridiculously long list of what I thought was important, like where he needed to work; where he needed to live, etc. I actually remember telling a co-worker about that, and seeing the look on his face when I was finished. He looked at me like I had farted. He squinted, his face was all puckered, and it was a little awkward. Needless to say, I still have a list, but it's a lot more realistic. I realize now what I deem truly important and, in my early 30's, I'm not only more certain of what I desire, but also of what I need.

I encourage you to use this "alone time" to really figure out what you want, and most importantly, what you need. We tend to look at alone time as the "pity party time."

Look at me; I'm a good girl.

I treat people right.

Why am I alone?

Why doesn't anyone see how great I am?

It's not fair!

I said it all before and meant every single word of it at the time. I even had people pump me up even more to tell me that I'm too good of a catch to be alone. "He's a fool," they would say. They would validate my deepest thoughts. Little did I know, I was being pruned to get what

I needed from the man of my future. Instead of boasting about how great you are, take this time to really get to know yourself. Trace back your dating history. Figure out what you did right and what you did wrong. Trust me, we all have things we may have done differently, if given the opportunity.

I try to keep in mind that "alone time" is much better than being "alone." "What's the difference?" you ask. Alone time should be a choice. When I get home after work, I enjoy walking in the door, throwing my keys on the counter, changing to comfortable clothes, then doing whatever it is I want to do. Whether its cook, order in, and sit in front of the television, or blast my favorite 90's tunes, I don't have to consider anyone or anything in those moments. They allow me to process the day and unwind. I know, when I get married, there will have to be modifications on my part, because I will be coming home to someone. Whether its cook dinner for us both, or make sure he has everything ready for work the next day, it will not all be about me.

Enjoy this single time you have to really get to know yourself and tweak the things you need to tweak. Our society likes to relish the notion that being single is a curse. You must have done something wrong! You can't keep a man or woman, and that's why you have been doomed to this fate. Don't believe the hype and lies. Take the time to take care of you, your mind, body and soul.

Usually after a breakup, I have taken time to pamper myself with massages, clothes, shoes, but also to not forget about my most important asset, which is my soul. I've learned I had to take care of that, too, because of the bruising it just took. Going to bible study, church service, reading a book, all can help you in the soul-care area. Just know that being alone isn't a curse, but a time to truly work on being all that God has called you to be. It is a decision you will not regret.

Chapter 8

The Social Network

Man, everyone wants the "tea," (also known as the gossip or the backstory). I know I touched on this earlier, but it deserved a chapter of its own. There is a difference between those who do not know the engagement is off and asking the status of wedding plans, versus those who have an idea, or know what is going on, and simply want the "tea." This will be another thing that will send you from 0-60 in a matter of seconds. Don't know the difference? Let me share a few helpful hints.

One of the initial ways you can discern if someone wants the tea is their first response to you telling them the engagement is off.

Those who want the tea will say, "Oh, what happened?" or, "Can you tell me why?"

Exactly. I know. How rude and insensitive.

After I just told you I made a life-changing decision, all you can say is why, or what happened? Someone who is genuinely concerned will FIRST want to know how you are doing. That does not mean that they don't want the details, but they first want to check in with you, to see how you are feeling, and if you are ok.

I cannot describe how much it meant for people to generally want to check in on me to see how I was. I felt like I spent so much time consoling others after their break-ups that it was refreshing to finally be on the receiving end of it.

Now, there are some people who ask how you are *just* to get the "tea." I had those who would initially ask how I was, but then immediately start asking for details. Like, "Now that I have you 'warmed' up, I can go in for the kill!" I have been blessed to have some friends who ask if I was okay and NEVER ask about the situation ever again. They just wanted to know if I was okay and then they left it at that. Jackpot! Not having to explain the whole story again was appreciated. Nothing says true friendship like that does.

I have one friend whom I speak to periodically, and more so in the past few years, because my ex and her ex are really good friends. I knew she had been through a divorce a few years back, and she could be someone I could talk to once, and if I felt up to it. Once I told her the engagement was off, she said she was sorry and asked if I was okay. She then asked if we could talk. I knew she wanted the "tea," but I was interested to hear what she had to say. She called the next day and, after explaining what happened, she offered praise for all I had accomplished and said she could relate, because of her situation. I knew that she could offer some insight and also provide me with a scripture to get me through. I was grateful.

People do not realize that during this time, it is just the small things that mean the most. Just like a discouraging word can change your day, an encouraging word has even more power.

I have another friend whom I talked to occasionally, and who texted me a few weeks after the ending of the engagement. I did not feel like explaining the scenario again that night, so I decided to wait until the next day to respond. It's important to know what triggers can change your day negatively, and to steer away from them. I knew that having to discuss the break up before I went to bed was just something that I wouldn't do anymore. I was so glad I decided to wait. The next day, when I finally responded, she wasted no time. After the initial, "How are you?" she went into how wedding planning was going. After I told her we were not getting married, her next question was, "Can I ask why?" She then proceeded to tell me how she followed him on Instagram and he didn't seem like himself.

There was no, "How are you doing? Do you need anything? I am here for you." Nothing. She later apologized for asking me to explain the situation over text, but offered nothing else.

Do you want to know my response?

Are you ready?

Wait for it, wait for it...

I told her to keep us both in prayer.

I know. Not sarcastic, mean, or even offensive.

In my mind I was thinking, "Now what kind of friend are you? I thought you cared? Is that all you really wanted?" To her defense, we were close many years ago and I did not think she intentionally was trying to be mean, but I felt her actions demonstrated at that moment all she was concerned about was being in the loop.

At work, there was a whole other group of "tea-ers." One male coworker had been gone for months and just never got wind of what had happened. He asked me about the wedding plans and I told him it was off, like I had told everyone else. He looked puzzled and confused, and walked off. I thought it was settled. The next day, he walked to my cube and said, "I gotta be nosy. What happened?"

I could applaud his honesty. At least he let me know what his intentions were. I politely said, "I'm not going to discuss it," and he walked off. Just like him, I was quick and to the point. About eight months had passed, so I was less annoyed but it did demonstrate that questions from others only bothered me if I allowed them to. Can you count on both hands, both feet and someone else's feet how many "tea-ers" you have in your life? I sincerely hope you do not have that many, but just know it comes with the territory. My advice is to not take it personally. I truly believe its human nature to be curious. How many of you watch reality TV? We want to be in the know about what is going on in the personal lives of others, especially celebrities, so is there much difference? Granted, we may not walk up to one of them and straight out ask them, but the curiosity is still there.

As we all know, the social network goes well beyond our network of co-workers. It also includes digital social networks we have as well. Social media can be our best friend and worst enemy. When things are going well, it can be a relationship dream. Liking their statuses, writing sweet notes on each other's wall or news feed. If a break up occurs, it turns into stalker century. From Facebook, Twitter, YouTube, and anywhere else where I could have been privy to RJ's information, I removed him. Once things ended, I temporarily deactivated my account on Facebook. The dreaded broken heart when you end the relationship on Facebook is the pits. Of course, when you change things, you get the texts and calls from people "eye hustling" to see what happened, and to add insult to injury.

My advice would be to take as much time as you need, but definitely take that break. Stalking his page will not help you move on. Every updated status from him is going to mean an eye roll for you, at least. You do not want to be tempted to reach out to him, or to feel worse about yourself if some girl likes a picture.

Going cold turkey from Facebook was, dare I say, refreshing? While it was supposed to be used for networking, it is usually used to be nosy and see who is with whom, why, where, and when. I did not feel that pressure, and it meant one last person I had to explain the story to.

In addition to deleting him, I unsubscribed to his closest friends and family. Unsubscribing is less harsh than deleting someone and allows you to still be friends, but not see status updates. To make matters worse, most of our friends were mutual, so I managed to narrow it down to about 10. Not having to see their updates or possibly see him tagged in post was what I needed. Like I said, I know it seems a little drastic, but canceling an engagement is dramatic, so whatever you need to do for you is what is necessary.

Despite someone else's actions, we must remember to always handle it like a lady and a child of God. It will be hard, but we cannot forget who we are and what we represent. I was once told that we go through things for someone else. Someone may reference how I acted today to determine how they will act in the future. My hope is that when they do, they will remember what peace and sophistication I had about it; how, despite my pain and hurt, I tried to take the high road and act Godly. How God's grace brought me from trial to triumph.

He deserves all the glory for how I am overcoming this situation and the only way I can do that is by acting as such. Trust me, you will be tested. Just know that in advance, and I believe it will help you when you encounter situations such as the ones I've shared. You must also believe that this too shall pass. Sometimes I wondered when the questions would end. It gave me peace knowing it would, and knowing that the next time I say I will get married, I WILL and to the greatest man made just for me.

Chapter 9

Can I Just Stay Here a While?

Do you know that feeling, when you are in your bed, under the covers, warm and cozy? Just when your dream is getting really good, whatever "good" is in your dream, the inevitable happens? Your alarm goes off! It startles you and pretty much shatters your dream to smithereens.

"Now, how can that be? How can my alarm clock be going off when I just closed my eyes? Don't I have at least another hour of sleep? Do I have to reach out from these warm, toasty covers and smack that little clock? Do I have to get up and face the day? But I was sleeping so well!" All those questions go through your head, even though you know all the answers.

That's how you have to look at your break up. Despite how good it feels to wallow in the hurt, to eat till you can't eat anymore, and to cry like it just happened an hour ago, you have to get up. You have to keep moving. I've realized that I've been blessed with the gift of channeling my anger and pain into something constructive. I have a few friends who deal with mental health issues in less-than-constructive ways, and their methods have made me acutely aware of times when I could have very well been in their shoes. I know it's not easy, but involving yourself in activities that allow you to get your mind off your problems, if only for a few minutes, can make a world of difference. Don't let sadness, depression, eating, shopping, crying and complaining be your comforter that you lay under, even though it feels good.

Just because being in the bed feels good doesn't mean we should stay there all day. We can't get much done under the covers, and soon we realize that it's not that bad outside of the covers, once we move around a little. Trust me, occupying your time with things of value will not only add to your life but possibly someone else's.

After my break up a year prior, I started to attend church on Friday nights. I also created a web series. I know, two opposite ends of the spectrum, but let me explain. In my relationship, we usually spent Friday nights together, so going to church was a great alternative. Not only did it feed my soul, but it also allowed me to start disassociating Friday nights with him. Friday night church attendance allowed me to take a deeper look at myself, and to worship with those who were just as broken as I was.

The web series actually came out of nowhere. I realized, at the time, that I wanted to write for a television show, but didn't know where to start. I felt like I didn't have the connections, and it would prove to be too difficult in the end. When I had just about given up, a colleague informed me about a friend of hers who actually worked in Hollywood and wrote for one of my favorite shows, "Girlfriends." My colleague gave me the writer's information and I reached out to him. He was extremely nice and encouraging, and he gave me some great advice. The best piece of advice he gave me was to write my own work and present it to the public in any way I could.

In the past, when he first began in the business, a writer had to have a structured portfolio of work, and had to enter festivals, hoping someone would notice his or her work. Now, with YouTube, Vimeo, and other video sharing websites, millions of people can see your work from the comfort of their own homes. You can also do your work from the comfort of your own home. That becomes your portfolio of work. The power is yours; you just have to use it.

Brilliant! His advice was priceless, and it spurred me to write 10 episodes of my web series, and then have 5 episodes produced. That was some of my proudest work, and all of it was created in a time of turmoil in my life. That "alone time" allowed me to think clearly, to really write from my heart. I realized that without the break up, I would have never thought about doing something like that. I learned there was always a silver lining in all we do; we just have to find it and cultivate it.

It didn't hit me in the face how much I liked to stay in my pain or frustration until I was in a heated discussion with a friend. We seemed to have had these heated discussions at least once every two weeks, but hey, that's what friends are for right? During that particular talk, I told him how frustrated I was because I felt I was often misunderstood. He said I was the one who was wrong, and he knew exactly where I was coming from. I continued arguing that he was wrong, and then he hit me with a bombshell.

He said, "Ericka, you like to play the victim. Woe is me; everyone thinks I'm this mean person. Blah, blah, blah."

What?

I just knew he was talking to an imaginary person behind me, because as strong as I am, I could never play the victim.

Wrong!

He hit the nail on the head. I was making myself a victim of my insecurity.

Deep, right? From a comment that would usually have sent most others and myself into a rage, I became more introspective, and I could see why he felt that way. I'm not going to lie. My initial reaction was what? Me? Victim? How dare you!

After I let it rest in my soul a little, I knew exactly where he was coming from. I felt justified in acting the way I did at times, because I figured I had the right. I would think, if only others could walk a day in my shoes, they would understand why I do what I do. I wasn't a full-out psycho to people, but when I felt compelled to go off on people, I did.

And I was justified, or so I thought.

My next interaction with that friend ran a lot smoother than that first one, because now I had *no* right to ever say, "I wish people would understand me in regards to my intentions."

I know there are some people who may never understand me, and I have come to the realization that it is ok. I cannot let their non-acceptance or misunderstanding cripple me. You shouldn't let whatever other people think or say about you do that, either. I choose not to stay a while in this state of being a victim. I know who I am, and whose I am. I'm going to continue to grow and not let my circumstances affect my attitude or actions.

Chapter 10

Christian Cringle

Dating? Just when you thought you wouldn't have to do that again, you are thrown back to the wolves. Well, not wolves, but the pack of men, out of which one may potentially be your next boyfriend.

When? How? Singles ministry? Online?

Where do you begin?

I had all those questions, and more. I wasn't sure what to do, or when it was appropriate to step back out there. I knew, for at least two months, I didn't want to date. Jumping right back into the dating game after such a traumatic event isn't the best. Trust me, you want to wait until you are ready.

You can't replace your ex, and you shouldn't try to. You want your new relationship to be fresh, new, and with as little baggage as possible. I knew that I had a lot of bitterness and anger I had to channel and get rid of before I could enter into another relationship.

Counseling helped me a great deal. Talking to your girls can be cool, but you may not get the clarity you need, because let's face it, they are your girls. They love you and support you; they want your ex to ultimately pay, to rot, and to be shamed for what he did. While that may make you feel better, it's not what you need to grow from the shattering experience you've had.

Since my job offered a few counseling sessions for free every year, I decided to go for it. I had used the service before, and I knew it would definitely come in handy this time around. I mentioned my counselor previously, and why we didn't connect, but she made a profound statement that stuck with me. She said that I usually went for spontaneous and fiery love, versus consistent and stable love. Whirlwind romances were usually how my relationships had begun, rather than my taking the necessary time to get to know someone more on a friendship level than a romantic one. Two months of dating before getting engaged, numerous love affairs that crashed and burned after only a month or two; it was a cycle that I didn't even realize I had been in. And there it was. Again. I was dating with a new game plan, and it wasn't going to be a whirlwind romance. It was going to end in true love this time around and, most importantly, it was going to take time to mature.

After about three months of going back and forth on the subject, I decided to give online dating a try. Most people didn't believe I needed that, because of how outgoing I've always been, but I thought it would be a nice way to streamline a new selection of potential suitors.

I knew the new *he* would have to be a spiritual, Godly man, so why not try Christian mingle? I signed up, but I was scared to put a profile picture up. Like someone would see me? What a hypocrite! I had told numerous friends that they shouldn't be afraid to try online dating, but I wasn't giving it an honest effort. After a few days with a profile, but without a picture and no hits, I decided to stop being stubborn and go all in. I put a picture up and, within minutes, I received numerous hits, and there was one guy in particular that I thought was attractive. I decided to send him a smile. We quickly began exchanging notes, and after about a week, he gave me his phone number. I was a little reluctant to call, but decided it was pretty harmless.

Our first conversation seemed like we had known each other for years. He was from Jamaica, and had a heavy accent that I thought was super sexy.

I know, bad girl! But hey, it was attractive.

We laughed and talked about our day and the upcoming weekend. I enjoyed his conversation, since it had been a while since I had talked on the phone with someone I was interested in. After texting all day on Easter Sunday, he suggested we meet. Again, I felt like maybe it was a little too fast. As comfortable as I felt during our phone conversations, I was a bit apprehensive about meeting him.

Would he be as cute in person as on his picture?

Was I being cat-fished?

Those thoughts, and a lot more, entered my mind; I wasn't sure what to do next. My friend assured me that it was just a meeting, and I needed to stop over-thinking it. Just get out there, right?

Fast forward to Tuesday. It was finally the night of The Date. I worked from home that day, so I had all day to prepare. Hair, clothes, smelling good. Had it all down, and I knew I looked beautiful.

I ventured to Midtown to a new dessert bar. I was still extremely nervous, but excited to meet him. I actually got there on time, and he was late, which pissed me off a bit. The dessert bar had been his idea but hey, Atlanta traffic can be crazy, so I decided to give him a pass. About 10 minutes later, he walked in and greeted me with a hug. His smile was inviting, and it just felt right. I relaxed, took a deep breath and was finally excited about what was to come during the evening. As we talked, the conversation flowed, but there were some questionable comments from him.

First, as random as our conversation topics were, he had the absolute nerve to question how a man could rape a woman with no weapon!

I know, right?

The dumbest thing you could ever hear.

To avoid an argument, I asked more questions, without trying to be judgmental, but his logic really threw me for a loop. The reality has been that men are innately stronger than women, which meant a man's body was a weapon in itself. As a woman who has feared for her safety, as well as feared being a victim of rape, I didn't think that because a man didn't have a gun, knife, or slingshot, that I could overpower him. I doubted, at six feet, two hundred and something odd pounds, he had ever feared being raped, so how could he even relate?

That was like me saying being circumcised wasn't that painful. Even after his idiotic comment, I didn't write him off, initially; I gave him the "no one is perfect" pass. Ah, but wait, the absurd comments weren't over.
Wait for it.

And....next, he proceeded to tell me he felt that women who had been with more than five partners were "sluts."

Right? Here again, I didn't run out of the restaurant. I didn't give him the, "Negro, *please!*" look.

I sat and smiled and asked more questions about why he felt the need to categorize women in that manner. Once again, I took the "No one is perfect" path, and added, "Everyone has a past." I threw in, "It's more important how you are deciding to live your future" and "Every saint has a past and every sinner a future."

Right?

He proceeded to tell me that it pretty much didn't matter and one's past was ultimately an indicator of the person they were... or, she was. Despite those few questionable remarks, I still felt like he was nice; he was cool to be around, but there were certain topics we should avoid. Clearly, there were.

Naïve of me?

You and your significant other don't have to agree on everything, do you? But I do feel you should be able to talk about anything. The more we discussed those topics, the more I should have known this was not a match made in Heaven, or even at the dessert bar. Our views were not just on different wavelengths, and in different spectrums, they were on different planets. I could tell by listening to him,

139

and talking to him, that he must have had an extremely sheltered upbringing, so sheltered that he only saw the world as black or white.

I left.

I left not really feeling like we just had an instant love connection, but trying to believe there might have been some potential for a connection, if some of his views changed. Mistake, mistake, mistake, mistake, mistake, mistake, mistake. A mistake! I should have cut my losses then and there and forever and ever. Nope! I thought I could "save" him. By" save," I mean "change" him.

We all know we have no power to change anyone, at least not permanently. Let's just say the feeling was not mutual. I called him the next day, and after small talk, asked him what he thought of me, since our first meeting. Boy, was I in for an earful! He proceeded to say he enjoyed my company, but he thought I was rushing into dating after breaking off the engagement with my ex. Mind you, he broke off an engagement three years prior, due to infidelity. He then said he could be off base with his assumptions, because of his previous situation, but that his gut told him we would just be "homies," but he could be mistaken.

I didn't know what all he was trying to say, but the one thing I did know was that he wasn't interested in me at all, and after that response, neither was I. My response to him?

"You should go with your gut," I told him. I mean, you would have thought that I had asked for his hand in marriage. I was livid! How could he? I thought that I had just hit the jackpot in really having something in common with the first guy I met online, just as friends first. I was not assuming it would end in marriage, or even a romantic relationship, but I didn't think it would end so abruptly.

Being judged by anyone is a horrible feeling, especially by a stranger, and especially because of such a sensitive topic. What I did learn, though, was to watch what I shared. In my attempt to be honest, I opened myself up to criticism. Special information should be reserved for special people. Lesson learned. On to the next one.

I had a list of criteria that I stuck by, and I didn't see anyone online that I felt I would gel with. What a snob I am, huh? Out of hundreds of men, there was only one I felt could be a possible love connection. I felt guilt about that, but I realized that I had to be true to myself. If my last encounter taught me anything, it taught me to go with my gut, just like the "Christian cringle" match at the dessert bar. He had been unapologetic about what he wanted and he knew I wasn't it. While I didn't respect his delivery, I respected what he said and even adopted it myself.

Within the first five minutes, I should have known that this would go nowhere fast! Instead, I had thought I should keep an open mind. That was my first mistake. I stuck to my guns, but eventually I deactivated my account, despite having two, paid months left. I felt like it was money wasted, but the $49 odd dollars I paid taught me a lesson I would carry for a lifetime. Know your standards and stick to them.

I ended up meeting the next man I would date for a few months on my own. I do believe there are some things you do have to compromise on because we are all different however, I knew what my non-negotiables were, and I knew I would stick to them. I decided to write them down after that incident and when I compared what I wanted with the man I was dating at the time, I realized that he fit most of things on my list, plus a little extra.

As I was watching Iyanla Vanzant, one of my favorite experts on relationships, family, and everything in between, she said something so poignant that it stuck with me. It was a segment on Oprah's *Lifeclass,* about "Daddy-less Daughters," and Iyanla discussed how the person you are with was who you thought you deserved to have, whether good or bad.

If you are with an amazing man who treats you like platinum, and supports you and your dreams, it was because you believed you could have a man like him in your life. If you were with a dream killer, who caused you constant angst and problems, it was because you believed you could only find a man like him too.

It didn't dawn on me, until that moment, that what you project is also what you will get in return. It's not merely by chance that you date those people, but it is a reflection of your self-worth.

How profound! I will keep that nugget with me, and I will know that whom I am with is a reflection of who I am.

I hope, despite my horrid experience with online dating, it's something you try if you are single and looking for something different. I don't regret the experience one bit and I am glad I tried it. It wasn't nearly as scary as I thought it would be, and it was actually kind of fun.

There are so many potential suitors out there that you may never run into if not for online dating. Always remember to be careful, though; let someone know where you are going and with whom. I've also had many friends who have had huge success with online dating so I would put my stamp of approval on it. Just make sure you don't compromise who you are to be with someone you don't really know.

Dating doesn't have to be Russian roulette; it can be like Spades. It's how you play your hand. If you feel you are at a point, after your engagement ends, you are ready to venture into the dating world, full steam ahead to you. Don't be timid; bust through that dating door like a bull! I mean that in the sense of you being open and ready for what will come. If it's online dating, know that you will encounter a few frogs before you meet your prince. If you don't, consider yourself blessed. If you do, consider yourself human. If you want to go the old fashioned route, and meet your potential suitor out and about town, go out. Try new things. In a major city such as Atlanta, we have plenty to do every night of the week.

Now, I'm not saying hang out at the bar all night, waiting for your Idris Elba. What I am saying is, don't limit yourself. Sites like meetup.com offer numerous options for meeting new people, without hitting up the club and bar scene. Focus on your interests and you will be more likely to find someone with similar interests.

When you do go out, don't take the neighborhood with you. You and your eight home girls may have a hard time meeting someone. Just like it's hard to meet decent guys, it's hard to approach a league of women. Bring your girlfriend who likes to have a good time, not the one who frowns often, looks people up and down, and couldn't have a good time if the food was free, the drinks were free, and there was a free car provided too. Have the mindset that you want to have a good time and you *will* have a good time. I truly believe that, what you think is what you receive. A good mindset goes a long way.

It's important to know that we will make mistakes in dating, but not too be so hard on ourselves. There are more fish in the sea where that one odd mackerel came from, so we must learn the lesson and move on. Quickly.

When I say quickly, I don't mean to the next "Joe" that you see. Make sure you don't dwell on it. No one walking this earth is perfect, so we have to know we will make mistakes. With affairs of the heart, we tend to beat ourselves up more than we should. One of the most important aspects of dating is to know that mistakes will be made. We just have to be strong enough to identify our weaknesses.

146

Chapter 11

Your First Wedding

We all knew the day would come. Despite feeling like our lives have stopped, actually, they haven't. Actually, they don't. While we want others to grieve with us and bring their own love to a halt, life just doesn't happen that way. While I was extremely happy about the wedding of one of my sorority sisters, there was a sting, a sharp sting. At one time, we tried to make sure our weddings didn't overlap. Then, one day, I was attending her wedding, excited and happy for her, but yet a little sad, knowing that I would have to wait a while until I would celebrate my own, happy, exciting day.

As I prepared for her wedding day, I decided I would not wonder, "What if?" I wouldn't reminisce about the plans I had made, or about what I wanted for my wedding. I would take the time to truly focus on their love, and I would celebrate them on their special day. At the same time, I was concerned that others would ask how my planning was going, because I hadn't told the rest of my sorority sisters what had happened. Thankfully, I wasn't hit with one question.

As I walked into the church that beautiful Saturday morning, I got a chance to peek at my sister, the bride, before she entered the church. She glowed. She looked absolutely beautiful. I saw her eyes, and then wiped a few tears from my own, and I knew it was going to be a wonderful day. It was a bit miraculous, in fact; it had rained all weekend, and was clear just before her big day.

Look at God!

The weekend was absolutely amazing, and I was able to catch up with people I hadn't spoken to in a while. I almost forgot about the place I had been in six months prior. I thought about how God continued to amaze me, and about the strength He gives us, that is like no other.

I know my "first wedding after" sounds easy. Others probably have horror stories about the first wedding they had to attend after their own broken engagements. I believe the most important thing to remember is to focus on the couple-to-be, as they marry. You can never go wrong if you can do that. If anyone tries to deflect the occasion on you and your situation, quickly bring it back. I know it may be easy to go off on a tangent about what he did wrong, trying to defend yourself and get your story out there, but trust me, in the end, it's not worth it.

I have witnessed a few instances where weddings depress people. The love they see in their bride or groom friends sometimes feels so far away. I truly believe, when we envy others, it's a fear that their happiness and bliss may never happen for us. I didn't realize that until I really sat and thought about it. At first, when I saw happy couples after my relationship ended, I found myself smiling, but then frowning. I thought about how happy they were and wondered why it was not happening to me. Sometimes, I found myself believing it couldn't.

Those kinds of feelings hit me especially hard during the holidays. I love my family gatherings, but wished I had someone to share the holidays with. During one Kwanzaa event, an engagement was announced, and I really felt it. I was one of the last few single ones there; I couldn't help but wonder when my turn would be. Watching my sister with her husband, who have a relationship that I truly admire, and because of the constant comparisons between her and me, made the fact that I didn't have a special someone that much more real.

There has to be a bright side to this right? I mean, with everything I have been through, and having to attend a wedding less than six months after I cancelled mine, what was there to look forward to?

Let me tell you. Everything!

After the weekend concluded, and I ventured out on my 12-hour trip back home, I was able to reflect on everything that I had experienced, and just how the weekend really had affected me. For one, it gave me hope. Witnessing their love made me realize the sacrifices we make for love and how love never fails. I was blessed to witness their relationship and some of the trials they had to endure, such as distance, and it was remarkable to see where they were on their wedding day. My perspective was, just as God blessed them to find each other, the same would happen to me. I was confident in that, sure of it even, and it was reassurance that my time would come.

My advice to anyone in this situation is to assess where you are. I know, if this wedding had been a month or two after the break up, I probably would have broken down. I think that is the worst thing one could do on someone's wedding day. Having a "moment" during someone's wedding can change the whole mood and can take attention away from the bride and groom. I had six months to pray, grieve, cry, and get counseling for everything that happened, so by the time my friend's wedding day came, I could safely say that I was in a good place.

I pray that the first wedding, post break-up, is as good for you as it was for me. If you feel you will not be able to handle it, do not be afraid to tell the bride and groom that you cannot make it. Hopefully, they will understand, and if they don't, they just don't. I'm sure they would rather have you cry at home than at they're wedding anyway.

151

Not to be left out of the arena of witnessing other couples' and friends' bliss, I would be remiss if didn't mention the first engagement I learned about, post break-up. About a month after the wedding of my sorority sister, one of my good friends texted me pictures of her engagement ring. I'm not going to lie and act like it didn't take me back just a little. I remembered sending out my own engagement ring text nearly a year earlier, and I remembered the joy I felt. I also remembered the text I got back, congratulating me. After my own engagement, the love from all of those who loved me, made the moment even sweeter.

In your post break-up time, the occurrence of someone's engagement is a little different from attending a wedding, because the information is coming specifically to you. You have it, and with today's technology, you can't act like you didn't get it. I'll revert back to my original advice on the situation. Don't think about yourself, think about the couple. In my case, they had been together for years and I was so excited for the new journey they were about to take. I knew the excitement she was feeling, and knew I would feel it again too.

Chapter 12
The Letter

The title sounds dramatic, huh? Well, I hope you aren't disappointed. This letter didn't explode; it wasn't even from RJ. It was actually a letter I had written to myself. Wait, wait. Chill.

Now, before you throw this book in the trash because you think I'm insane, let me plead my case. A few months back, my friend invited me to a women's public health meeting that was about women's empowerment and networking. I met some amazing women and was inspired in more ways than one. One of the last things we did, to conclude the meeting, was to write a letter to ourselves, about goals and desires we wanted to accomplish within the next six months. We each had an orange postcard that we addressed to ourselves. I thought the idea was brilliant!

As I wrote my postcard, tears started welling in my eyes, because I was expecting God to heal my heart and bless me, personally and professionally. I knew that He was more than able to fulfill my heart's desires. As the weeks after the meeting turned into months, the letter fell off my radar, until about two weeks prior to its arrival. By that point, I was a little nervous; I began to wonder and speculate about the exact date the letter would arrive. Truthfully, I had forgotten most of what I had written, until I sat down and thought about it for a few minutes. Actually, I only remembered what I wrote at the top of my list; I wrote about meeting my future husband, who would be a God-fearing man.

Yes, you're probably, like, how could you even think about that at this point?

Did you forget the heartbreak you just experienced?

Why do you want to rush into something so soon?

I need to be clear. I *didn't say* I wanted to be engaged or even married in six months; I just said that in six months from the time I wrote the letter, I wanted to *meet* the man I was going to marry. Because of everything that I had experienced, I had found clarity about what I wanted. I knew that the love in my heart would blossom

154

into something that would last forever, next time around. Remembering that made me realize how good God is, and how He answered prayers.

Two weeks later, I received the letter. It was a beautiful Sunday morning and, since I had not checked the mail in the last two days, I just saw a bunch of junk mail at first. As I began to sift through it, and sort what to keep and what to throw away, I saw that familiar orange post card. I was so excited to see it I almost threw all the other mail that I had in the trash. At that moment, that was the most important piece of mail I had ever received. I was more than ready to open it and read what I had been praying for, and see how things had transpired in the past six months. I made sure that there were no distractions, such as TV and cell phones around and I excitedly opened the letter.

As I read it, I cannot lie, I was not as emotional as I had been when I was writing it six months earlier, but I was thankful that I was not in the same mind space I had been in back then. I had been feeling so broken at that time that I was really crying out in that letter. I knew every good work God started, He would finish. I had more faith, six months later as I read my own words. I knew that I was right where I needed to be. I was dating someone, and while he didn't turn out to be my husband, he helped me learn a lot about myself, and about more of what I desired in a husband. It just proved, once more, how real God is and how He hears us, even when we don't think He does.

I would like to adopt this exercise with my girlfriends. I think it is good to put what we want on paper, and then, maybe six months later, have the ability to reflect back on what our priorities were, as well as the goals we were looking to pursue. Writing a letter like that also continues to prove just how faithful our God is. I didn't necessarily get everything I desired and had written on my postcard, but I did get everything I needed, which was, and still is, even better.

I think it's something you should try, especially if you feel you are at a crossroads in your life. My postcard is currently sitting on my mirror, on top of my dream board. Looking at it every day continues to assure me that brighter days are ahead, and not just because of the bright orange color of the postcard.

Chapter 13

Someone New

To be honest, I thought I would have dated a lot more before I had a new boyfriend. I actually had only been on two dates before we started to get serious and it was totally unexpected. I met him at an Urban League meeting, and I was immediately captivated by his energy. He blazed through the room briefly, and talked about how he was rushing to make the meeting after attending his grandfather's funeral. I've never seen anyone have so much peace about attending a funeral, but he truly seemed happy to be with us at that moment. I turned to my friend and said, "I like him."

As romantic as that sounds, things didn't go as planned. I didn't talk to him and immediately get swept off of my feet. I waited for the crowd to leave, and introduced myself. I smiled, I was warm and inviting, and I was sure that he would want to take me out the next night. NOT!

He thanked me for coming and told me where to submit my email to get more updates on where the meetings would take place in the future. Our conversation was kinda dry, very formal. I know it was a general meeting, but dang! I thought he would surely ask me for my number, or at least ask me to come to the happy hour that was being held next door.

Well, I didn't give up so easily. I went to a meeting that was about two weeks later; I made sure to dress my best. When I walked up, he was in his car, and he said the meeting had been moved. Still very professional. Throughout the entire meeting, I spoke, as did others, and then the meeting ended. I was a little disappointed, but I saw another cutie at the meeting, so I wasn't too concerned anymore about the first guy.

Well, it wasn't over yet.

So there was another meeting at the Young Professionals Urban League headquarters. I needed training for an upcoming community service event but, for some reason, I couldn't find the building and didn't know what to do. I remembered he sent the email about the event, so I called his cell phone to get directions. I didn't really think much of it. Later that evening, he asked for my phone number, and we began communicating every day after that. He told me he was a personal trainer, and said he would agree to work out with me.

Those who know me know that I try to bum free workouts when I can, so I was all for that! The cutest thing happened next. He told me that he really wasn't a trainer, but needed to find a way to spend more time with me!

I know you are smiling from ear to ear now.

I sure was. It was one of the sweetest gestures I had experienced in a while. We began working out in the mornings, and began to build a beautiful friendship.

Soon after, we started dating exclusively and, while I can't lie, it was a bit scary. It was nice to have had someone to spend time with and grow with. I promised myself I would take this one-day at a time, and I had really been sticking to that. He would definitely have liked the relationship to move faster, but I promised myself I would take my time. We all know, now, what happens when I don't!

I can honestly say that at a time in my life when I didn't feel like I was enough, he made me feel like more than enough. In my relationship with RJ, I always felt like he would see my worth in the way I supported his career, and in all the things that he loved. Ultimately, I was sacrificing my desires for the greater good of our relationship. That may not always be a bad thing, but when you feel that person will not reciprocate, that's when the resentment builds.

In my new relationship, I felt that he accepted me more, just as I was, and he didn't expect me to do anything but strive for my own dreams. He not only encouraged me, but he also bought my school supplies for my first screenwriting class. Matter of fact, he found the class, and actually put me in contact with those who had similar interests.

He was also a dreamer; he knew, one day, he would be a Division 1 basketball coach. He knew it, believed and talked about it, often. Because he was so confident in his purpose, he did anything he could to help me achieve mine.

Ladies, you never know where and when you will find that special someone. I prayed for a man like the one I had, and I wasn't quite sure what to do, once he came. You must be aware that God answers prayers, and you never know when, so be careful what you pray for. He just may give it to you, and sooner than you expected.

As much as I prayed, I still was scared of possibly falling in love again. He was very patient, and continued to talk me through my past hurts, while still helping me prepare for my future, spiritually, mentally, physical and emotionally. I knew he really cared for me deeply, but I promised myself that I wouldn't rush into anything, no matter how good it felt.

Even with all the quality time we spent together, and the fun times we experienced with each other, we had our problems, like there are in any other relationship. I can honestly say, that since we both decided to be abstinent until marriage, it truly allowed us to work through our problems.

I know you want to close the book now, but please don't. Hear me out. Being abstinent has been one of the best decisions I could have ever have made. It has allowed me to date with a clear head, and a clear heart. As much as we enjoyed each other's company, we debated often. I chose "debate," rather than "argue," because they weren't petty arguments. You know what I mean, petty arguments about you calling me at 9:45 instead of 9:30. They were debates on future life goals, such as the life we wanted to have with our families, and the importance of setting family traditions etc. Oftentimes, they turned into three- to four-hour conversations, and while we may not necessarily have seen eye to eye, we did understand more of where the other person was coming from.

Our relationship had seen twists and turns, but we've managed to iron them out with communication. I believe one of the reasons for that is because we weren't intimate, physically. The mental intimacy that we shared was like no other relationship I had ever been in. My sister jokes that we have "serious talk" every day, and sometimes it feels that way. I realized I would much rather talk every day about our issues, than skirt around them, or cover them up with sex.

I can't lie and say I don't miss sex, but I realize that, the next time I have sex, it will be with my husband, the man I will be with forever, and it won't just be sex, it will be love with my soul mate.

Question for you: Have you tried abstinence?

Have you ever thought about it?

After one relationship in particular, that left me asking why we did not work out, I realized I wanted God to pick my mate; I wanted to try dating His way. If you are thinking about, I suggest you give it a try. It has to be something you are truly committed to, so if you decide to make this choice, I commend you. We give enough of ourselves when dating, why not save yourself, physically, for the one who will be ultimately deserving, your husband.

When seriously considering dating someone, it's important to note that there may be some residual emotions left over from the break up. This does not necessarily mean that you still have feelings for your ex, but more so, it means you have feelings you didn't get a chance to express, or you have feelings you didn't even know you had. Now, I know I talked earlier about counseling in regards to getting out all your feelings, and dealing with them to avoid this very thing, but through time, I realized that certain emotions come up only after you have begun a new relationship. Confusing? Yes. Real? Indeed.

Chapter 14

1 Year Post-Proposal

My saying for this past year has been, "Time flies." When I got engaged, I thought my nearly two-year engagement would be like watching paint dry. I just felt it would be forever until I would say, "I do" to the man that I thought I would spend the rest of my life with. I was so wrong!

This year has flown by, and the one-year anniversary of my proposal crept up on me like a 10-year high school reunion. You wonder, "Has it been that long already?" I remember it like it was yesterday. I could not believe it. Initially, I thought I would be sad, thinking about the details of the proposal. How happy we were, the plans we had, and just the excitement of planning a life together.

Boy, was I wrong. It was a regular day for me, one year later. Instead of thinking about how sad I was that our plans had not panned out as we originally hoped, it was full of thought of how much I have grown and learned from the mistakes that I made leading up to the engagement. On this engagement anniversary day, my sister, brother-in-law, and I, took my mother to the airport after her weeklong stay here in Atlanta. I was sad to see her go, but excited to get back in the swing of my regular routine.

My sis and I went to the store and got a few groceries and things for the house. As we walked out of one of our favorite stores, I just looked at her said, "I am sure glad I'm staying." Had the engagement still been on, I would have been in the process of selling my home, looking for a new job, and moving across the country to California.

She smiled at me and said, "Me too! We would not have been able to do things like this much longer."

She later followed that up with, "You were all in, too. You were ready to go."

It hit me like a ton of bricks. I had been ready to practically uproot my whole life, and to move where I knew no one but my husband. I had been okay with it and, to be honest, a little excited about a new beginning. I could not tell my sister all of that, but it reminded me of the head space I had been; how just a year ago, I had been ready to move.

I cringe at the thought of it now.

I did not dwell on this for days, but it made me consider how strong I had become. My dream was to be near family, mainly my sister, to see my nieces and nephews grow up and vice versa, because my sister and I never had that experience. My sis and I also said we wanted to be next-door neighbors, but I think that was just pushing it. The fact that I would have sacrificed my dreams for someone else's made me realize I was not ready to be married, because I would not have been happy. RJ said that to me when he was explaining his reservations for not continuing with this engagement, but I just assumed it was his nerves. I did not really think about it from his perspective. He said I would resent him, somewhere down the line, and I thought I would resent him more for not wanting to marry me. A year later, I realized moving to California would have helped fulfill his dream, not mine.

It is so vital to go back and analyze events that have happened to you after time has passed, because you are now probably in a different space mentally. Now, this is ***not*** a time to play the songs that remind you of him, or watch the movie you enjoyed so much together. This is ***not*** a memorial. It should be a process, not only to exemplify your growth, but also to think of the role you played.

Could you have prevented something? Did you ignore the signs? In my case, I realize there had been a lot of things I could have done differently. That's not to say I would have changed anything that happened, but in the future, I know I will try not the repeat the mistakes of my past.

First, our relationship was really a whirlwind. Despite being friends for so long, we only dated for two months. Regardless of knowing someone for over half of your life, dating him is a whole other arena that we hadn't explored. We were just getting to know each other, as boyfriend and girlfriend, before accelerating to matrimony. Second, our priorities weren't the same. My focus was family; his was career. Despite the love we had for each other, we both had different agendas, and they conflicted often.

Third, we let love lead.

No, that's not a typo! We let our love for each other lead our actions, which was a huge red flag. We must remember, love is an emotion, and emotions can make us laugh, cry, and do other things that are the complete opposites of each other. Logic didn't kick in until much later; by that time, we had already moved too fast and too far.

Love is *not* all we need for everything to succeed.

Let me say that once more.

Love is *not* all we need for everything to succeed.

There are plenty of other factors that make a great recipe for a great marriage. I suggest not only sitting down with each other, before marriage, to discuss finances, children and child rearing, and spirituality, but also speaking to a counselor or marriage therapist.

ALTARcation

I have learned I would rather be more than prepared for getting married, than have to end an engagement after it had already begun.

Chapter 15

Thrive Not Survive

One of the most profound phrases I've heard most recently, came out of a casual conversation with a girlfriend of mine. Despite the breakup that my friend had just gone through, her counselor recognized her strength, but told her that it was not good enough to just simply get by. As women, we are built with the strength of getting through many hardships, while ensuring that the home is always taken care of.

Husband or baby's father leaves?

Home still taken care of. Food is still on the table and the kids still have clothes on their back.

Laid off? Home still taken care of. Hustling doing side jobs, and whatever else needs to be done for the bills to be paid.

No raise this year? Home still taken care of. Stretching money in numerous ways, so no one even notices that you are struggling. Sound familiar? We do it every day, and most of the time without a second thought.

After my dad left, my mother worked harder and longer hours, but we didn't skip a beat. My mother made sure my sister and I had everything we needed and most of what we wanted. That's what women do. I never thought there could be anything wrong with that picture.

I recently talked with a co-worker, which affirmed the counselor's sentiments on the "thrive not survive" theory. This colleague called me up, one particular day, to vent, but also to talk about her growth. She said something so profound to me that I initially took as a compliment, but later wondered if it truly was.

She said, "Ericka, I used to look at you, and you would always smile, and no one would ever know if you had a care in the world."

I immediately smiled (even though we are over the phone) and thought, "Wow, I'm so glad people can always see me smiling. I'm glad people don't know my personal life."

She wanted to take a page from my book and I felt honored. If that conversation would have never taken place, I don't know if I would have ever thought that I was anything more than a survivor. I thought that was the ultimate accolade. It felt so opposite of being a victim that I was ok with that. That particular night, what she said really stuck with me. The next day, when I attended church, it was reiterated once again.

We had just started this series titled, "40 Days of Faith," and I was excited about what would happen at the end of the 40 days. I felt like my faith was in a good place, but could stand to grow some. My pastor discussed that, during times of trial, you can't just go through the motions, but you have to be expectant of your breakthrough. You have to rejoice that your season is coming. The ultimate would be to help others during your time of need.

My mouth nearly hit the floor. That's it!

When I arrived home, I thought about what I did when I was enduring a trial. Was I just surviving? Going through the motions? Maybe smiling on the outside but dormant on the inside? During my first break up, a year prior to breaking off my engagement to RJ, I dove into creating a web series. I was proud of my work, not only because I created it, but because I created it within the space that I did. I had felt so low at that time; I didn't know what I had done to deserve what happened.

It was a break up, yes, but my ex threw everything but the kitchen sink at me. He brought up events that happened months prior, and unloaded them all at once. I felt bullet-riddled when he walked out of that door. Yes, I put work into something else to get my mind off of it, but was I truly helping others? Or was I simply working for my own good?

Fast forward a year later. Not more than a week after I ended my engagement to RJ, a friend called and told me that another friend of ours was in the hospital. He was not in great shape, and she wanted me to visit him in the hospital. Initially, I thought about all I was going through,

174

and did I even have the energy or even the emotion left to give to someone else? I really wanted to have a pity party for myself for at least a few weeks. Was that too much to ask?

After my sister and a friend went to the hospital to see him, we realized just how severe it was. He was in the ICU and didn't look much like himself. My sister said she almost cried when she saw him. At that moment, it made me realize that the present moment was bigger than myself. Despite what I was going through, it was nothing, compared to what our friend was enduring. He was fighting for his life. While my heart may have been hurting, I was physically well, and that was a blessing within itself.

In that moment, I realized that life is bigger than me. I had to help my friend, even if that only meant having others pray for him. Praying for someone else, despite how I was feeling, allowed me the feeling to truly thrive, and not just survive.

When you think you have nothing left to give, and you find it in you to give a little bit to someone else, that's God.

That's faith.

That's living.

Our friend is doing so much better now, but he has a long road of recovery ahead of him. I realized, at that moment, that God has never given me more than I could bear, and I was more than a conqueror. He blessed me with life, health, and family who supported me. So while I may have been feeling down, there was definitely someone else out there who was in worse shape than I was. I had to count my blessings daily, and really be appreciative and more cognizant of what I had, rather than what I felt I was lacking.

Another point the counselor brought up was that, in simply surviving, you aren't really dealing with your situation, you are merely going through the motions. I encourage you take the time and find someone to talk to. Whether it be your minister at church, or a counselor that you haven't met yet, it's important to find someone to help you deal with everything that is going on.

I know counseling is extremely taboo, especially in the African American community, but I do believe it is extremely beneficial. I've also decided that I need to feed my soul and my faith, just like any other parts of my body.

Ecclesiastes 6:7 states, "We work hard to feed our appetites; meanwhile our souls go hungry."

Our souls are the only things that we will have in the afterlife, so it's vital that we feed our souls, daily. For myself, I bought a devotional to spend that alone time with God every day. For you, it may be meditation. Whatever it is, make sure your soul is fed and fed well.

It's no use starting a good relationship when the timing is bad. Compare it to eating a gourmet dinner on dirty plates. Yes, the food looks good, but once you eat long enough to see how dirty the place is underneath it, you will wish you hadn't eat it at all.

Within the last year, I realize that everything that I have gone through has been for someone else. Sometimes it's a hard pill to swallow, but it gives me some sort of comfort. When my engagement ended, I immediately went into the mode of who am I going through this for? What friend do I have now, or will I have in the future, that will need my experience to help them with there's? I know that through everything there is a testimony. The question remains, what will your testimony be? Will it be of a victim or victor? In the past, I was blameless. Everyone had done everything to me, and I truly didn't deserve the treatment I was getting.

Isn't that nice?

Isn't it empowering? Feeling like someone wronged you for no apparent reason almost gives you a high. I mean, not a literal high but it makes you feel like you can walk around feeling that the world owes you.

I truly believe that being the victor means realizing your own faults in any situation. Now, don't get me wrong. There are certain situations where there is only one to blame, however, I do believe, in many situations, we can

178

take a look back at ourselves to discover not only what our role in the situation was, but we can learn a lesson on what not to repeat.

Another question you should consider is, "How do you view yourself?"

Does everyone you meet know your break up story – verbatim -- because of how often you've talked about it?

I truly believe your words have power over your future, so speak life.

Yes, your engagement is over, but that doesn't mean that you won't ever be engaged or married. With faith, we know this and understand this, so we have to stop talking about our break-ups. I know we usually think that talking about issues in our lives makes us feel better. It can, but speaking only of it, constantly, and getting as mad as you were the day it happened, isn't healthy.

You aren't thriving, you're lying to yourself. Give yourself a deadline of how long you will talk about the cancelled engagement. You can revisit it if you feel you can offer advice to someone about a similar situation, but if it's just a rant about your anger, don't do it.

I remember the weekend after I called off the engagement, I went to dinner and laughed and smiled like nothing happened. By remembering the looks on my friend's faces, I knew that they were stunned by my reaction. I knew they were waiting to have a big, sit down, rant fest, like we usually did, but I knew it wasn't healthy for me at that time. I needed to escape my feelings for that moment and, once I got home, I cried like a baby, but was glad I made it through at least another dinner. Eventually, my girls and I discussed it, but it was on my time, and in my way. It wasn't with everyone, all at once, because I know how we as women can be. Instead, it was more to inform them of what happened, not to get their opinions of the situation. That made it easier for me and, once the next girlfriend suffered a break up, I was able to give advice that helped her thrive through the difficult times. She knew, from my past, that I was accurately sharing my experiences.

Realizing your worth is another way to thrive during this difficult time. For me, I knew that I deserved a man who was 100% sure about desiring to marry me. That was the determining factor in whether to hold on, or to dissolve the engagement. If you are fresh out of a break-up, and feel like you are just going through the motions, ask yourself this question:

"What do I deserve?"

I know it sounds simple, possibly mundane, but you have to be truthful to yourself. I believe recognizing and appreciating what you're worth coincides with your self-esteem. If you were the one who broke off the engagement, you have the distinction of knowing that you are worth more than what you were getting, so you should applaud your choice and never question it.

Dr. Laura Schlessinger wrote in her book, Bad Childhood-Good Life: How to Blossom and Thrive in Spite of an Unhappy Childhood:

"You should not be satisfied with being a victim, nor with being a survivor. You should aim to be a conqueror. There is an extraordinary quality of spirit that

leads one to aspire to conquering rather than surviving. I hope you discover that spirit in yourself."

I believe many women who are going through a break-up are in survival mode, trying to get through the minute, hour, and the day; praying for light at the end of the tunnel. We carry the scars of shame, guilt or even disappointment at failing at something, regardless of who is to blame.

A conqueror mindset is one of control, of someone who doesn't let her circumstances dictate her mindset or future. I urge you who are reading this to shake off the shame and embarrassment of this failed relationship, and to know that you are a force to be reckoned with.

You are of value, and you are truly an overcomer. This situation may have shaken you, but it won't break you, if you don't give it the power.

I now ask, which one are you? The victim or victor?

Chapter 16
Marrying Your Father

I'm sure I'm one of the many women in America who tunes in to Iyanla Vanzant's "Fix Your Life" on the Oprah Winfrey Network. On this specific episode, Iyanla, spoke to parents who didn't agree with who their daughter had decided to marry. Iyanla, in her Iyanla way, discussed that the man the daughter was marrying was a reflection of her father. Thinking I had heard this all before, I was about to run downstairs to get a glass of water, when Iyanla dropped the bomb.

Not the f-bomb or some other elicit word, but the bombshell that set fireworks off in my head. She went on to explain that the man their daughter was marrying was her father, whether it was who he was, who he is, or who she wants him to be.

She left the parents to stew, simmer, and marinate in this epiphany.

After I picked my jaw up off the ground, I grabbed a cup of water, but as I walked back up the stairs to where the television set is, I began to realize just how true the statement was.

The episode, not to mention Iyanla's pronouncement, caused me to think of my relationship with my father. When I was growing up as an adolescent, there was no man on Earth better than my dad. He was my superman. There was no one who could hurt me as long as daddy was there. My sister and I looked up to our dad, literally and figuratively, as if he were the king of the world, in addition to being head of our household.

My dad was also one of the funniest people you could ever hope to meet. I believe it is from him that I got my wit. He always made my sister and I laugh, and the neighborhood kids loved him, too. He was young, hip, and easy to relate to. My mother was more of the disciplinarian, so Daddy would always help get us out of trouble, which would oftentimes get him in trouble with my mom. My dad didn't care though. We were "Daddy's little girls," and nothing could change that, or so I thought.

It's almost taboo now, to live in a two-parent household, where your biological parents are still together, but growing up in the late 80's and early 90's, it was my norm. Most of my friends in the neighborhood lived with both parents, and I was just like them. While my family wasn't "the Huxtables," and in fact, neither of my parents had a college degree, we had a lot of love in our home. Our parents instilled in us how vital college was, and how we were going to attend, no questions asked. The same could be said for many kids in our neighborhood, and even for my close friends in high school. In our own perfect world, we would graduate high school, go to college, get married, and live in neighborhoods identical to the ones where we grew up. That was our vision.

By the time I got to high school, the vision wasn't just blurry, it was derailed.

As I was entering high school, my father left for an assignment for work and never returned. In fact, he didn't make it to work, either. To be honest, I don't know where he went, but he never came back to live with us. About two years prior, I learned of my father's drug use, but in my mind, I thought things would get back to normal soon enough. After my sister and I found out about his drug use, by eavesdropping on a phone call between my parents, my world came crashing down. The man I looked up to, who I thought could do no wrong, was somehow imperfect.

I didn't know what to do. I thought I could fix him. Then came the blame.

Maybe he started using drugs because I didn't spend enough time with him, or so I thought. I made an effort to go straight home after school, and to spend as much time with him as I could. Sometimes, I thought it worked. He would leave for a few days, but he would always make it back home before the week started. He never missed work, so I felt I could always count on him, to some extent. After a year or two, he would still go to work, but he wouldn't come home. I assumed, because we didn't move, the bills

186

were being paid and all was as well as it could be. I never saw my mom cry, so I assumed she was fine, too.

Life kept moving on until that fateful day that summer after a trip to Disney World with the drill team I participated in. When the magical life I had encountered in that magical place, and actually thought I had been living, just halted as soon as we got home.

After someone from my father's job kept calling and leaving messages that he was AWOL (absent without leave in the military), I knew things would never be the same again. My mother did what mother's do; she stepped up to the plate. She didn't skip a beat, either. Some days, she worked 20 hours, to ensure my sister and I would not have to alter our lifestyle. We started high school, and acted as if nothing had happened. We lied to friends when they asked where our father went. We were too embarrassed to say that our family was no longer like those in the neighborhood. Our "Huxtable" family was now just an illusion. Little by little, my sister and mother and I informed the neighbors of our new family unit -- our mother, my sis and me.

After the years of secrets, I believe we were finally happy to be honest about our situation. My sister and I still earned good grades, won Homecoming Queen, and Prom Princess, and got accepted to one of the top five public colleges in the nation. Life was good, real good. I didn't realize that I hadn't actually processed what had happened. My father left the house, and we continued as if a major shift had not occurred, a family member was not absent. A whole song was missing from that album I called high school, and without that song, the other tracks were good, but it wasn't great anymore.

Dating was also interesting in high school. My mother was adamant about my not dating until I was 16. I could go on group dates with guys, but no one-on-one action was going down. You may think, just have your man meet you at the group date outing, and *voila,* magic. We'd found the loophole and, boy, did we use it! Often. Even so, I couldn't have guys call the house until I was 16. That proved to be a bit more challenging. I would just call most guys and remind them to never call me. You would also think that we found the loophole in that, but that meant the guy was at my beck-and-call, and they didn't like that

188

much. Still, I had plenty of guys who were interested in me. Once I turned 16, I was able to have guys come over while my mom was home and that's when things got interesting.

My mother was and is a sweet woman. She would greet the guys who introduced themselves when they came over. Oftentimes, they would bring her flowers to show how "innocent" they were, and my mother's face would light up. They would almost be fooled into thinking they could get away with anything.

Once they did anything remotely wrong to momma's baby, (i.e. me), my mother would forbid them to come back, which forbid me from talking to them ever again. It was an early lesson I learned, that if I wanted to keep dating them, I would have to keep their indiscretions to myself, because they soon learned that my "Momma didn't play that."

Ok, now back to high school. I dated a lot. I wasn't promiscuous by any stretch of the imagination, because I did not, in fact, lose my virginity until my senior year of college. I learned, through my mother, that when guys did me wrong, they were gone. I didn't tolerate much; I sent quite a few guys packing. Coming back was not an option either.

Once they showed they weren't interested, I made sure (with the help of my mother) that things were completely over. Not even platonic. I think that was the part that kept their mouths hanging wide open.

"We can't be friends any more either? Dang!"

Yup, that was me. I did this often to men that I dated, and it still holds true today to an extent. I don't speak to too many of my exes except for one. I didn't realize that I received that trait from my mother until I sat down and reviewed my dating history. Men didn't have a chance, when they messed up.

I also made a pact with myself that I didn't want to date anyone like my dad.

I know, harsh huh?

Despite my dad being my pride and joy as a child, if a guy reminded me of my dad, he got the axe. More specifically, if the guy reminded me of my dad's drinking. My father was also an alcoholic, but not the raging alcoholic like you see on television and the movies. My father had a cool Heineken every night, and for the longest, I thought it was normal. I didn't realize that everyone didn't drink every day. My dad also went to work every day too, so I just assumed it was ok.

I didn't realize my dad was a functioning alcoholic until I was sick one day, and happened to read a pamphlet at the base hospital. It gave some of the signs of alcoholism and, as I read those signs, they sounded too familiar.

Drinking daily. Check.

Drinking alone. Check.

Drinking in the morning before eating. Check.

I recall asking my mother about it, and she said she wasn't sure, but to leave the pamphlet on the kitchen counter for my dad to see. I remember leaving it, but my dad never said anything about it. Neither did I.

After he left, I wondered how he could leave his precious wife and children, and not wonder if they were eating or even alive. I didn't understand it. I vowed I would never date a man who could do that. If he had more than one drink while we were out, he would get the boot. I think I made men I dated feel like they were an alcoholic, because I was the monitor of their drinks. It wasn't until after college that I realized some people drink responsibly. Even so, the drinking trait was something I was very adamant about avoiding.

In early 2012, my counselor asked me about the relationship I had with my dad. I didn't understand why. What did that have to do with my ex breaking my heart? We need to stick to the subject at hand, was what I was thinking. The counselor probed more and more, and in between tears, I told him about my relationship history with my dad. My dad re-entered my life during my junior year of college, and while we're on speaking terms, we aren't as close as we were when I was a child. Still, I didn't know what that had to do with why I was there, crying at the counselor's office. My counselor then asked me if I considered my relationship with my dad a factor in my

192

relationship with men. I didn't at the time. I thought they were unrelated, but little did I know, I was dating my dad, or who he used to be.

I asked my dad to come visit, but didn't tell him why. I was afraid that he wouldn't come, more out of fear or rejection, and at that point, I couldn't take rejection from another man. My dad doesn't like to talk about what happened during that time in his life after he left the family and I thought the counselor could reach my dad in a way that I couldn't. My dad didn't end up coming until the next year, and by that time, I had been engaged and single again, and didn't have the counselor's information to contact him for a session.

I decided, on this particular night with my dad, that I would be the counselor. Bad idea. After a night out on the town with a few libations, I decided to tell my dad my previous plans about us seeing the counselor, and how we needed to talk about what happened in the past, to help with my future relationships. Let's just say it was bad timing. We argued all the way home. He later apologized for what he said, but he made a statement that made me understand him, and the situation, a little better. He told me, close to tears, that he did the best that he could. My father was only 19 when my sister and I were born, and he decided to enroll in the military to give our family a better life. For that, I will always be grateful. For the majority of my life, my father provided.

I started to look at who my father was, rather than who he wasn't. Doing that made me realize how wonderful my dad really is. It's easy that when you are wronged, you can only see the bad, and not the good, in someone... the hurt and not the joy. Truth be told, I can't say that, because of my father's actions, I had a bad life. I actually had an amazing childhood. I know that there are some traits in men that I will avoid with regard to choosing a husband, but I know there are many traits about my dad that are admirable, and that I would love for my future husband to have, as well.

Still thinking about what Iyanla said, I wondered just who I had been dating throughout the years. Was it more of who my dad was? Or was it who I wanted him to be? I took inventory. I had a few more epiphanies. I truly believe that I dated two parts of my dad. Who he was, and who I wanted him to be. I also had to reconcile that who he is, was no longer who he was. The man that I grew up with had gone through changes, and I'm sure many other things that I am not aware of, which was the hardest thing for me to understand. Just like I'm not the 14-year-old girl I was when he left our lives. I was holding my dad to a standard of being someone he couldn't be, and at times, I was holding my boyfriends or potential suitors to a role they couldn't fill.

One of my favorite songs from Mary J Blige's *The Breakthrough* album is *"Father in You."* The first time I listened to it in my car, by the time I got to my destination, my eyes were red and puffy from crying. I didn't realize that, in the men I was dating since I was an adult, I yearned for the father in them. Whether it was the affection, acceptance, and just hoping they wouldn't abandon me, I inadvertently yearned for the father in them, and when the relationship was over, a part of me felt like they were abandoning me, like I felt my father had abandoned me as a child.

I had to come to terms with the fact that I only had one father. The issues with him had to be resolved before I could have a long-lasting, successful marriage with any other man. Now by resolving, I don't mean sitting down with coffee or tea, laughing after a few "I'm sorry's," or even my father apologizing for everything that he has done. It was more important to recognize the resentment I had towards my father and resolve, within myself, that I had to forgive and accept him for the man he is today.

Our conversation that night didn't go as planned, and while I didn't feel that he truly understood where I was coming from, or why I was so hurt, I did realize that I couldn't keep blaming my dad for the past. I believe true forgiveness, while it is not forgetting, is in not bringing up the incident again. It is not reliving it, if another issue occurs. I found myself saying I forgave my dad, but when his name was brought up, I would roll my eyes, or tell the stories of what my dad didn't do.

That's not forgiveness. I was still upset. Even after our conversation that night, I called my sister and I was still angry. While my dad and I ended the night with a hug, after about two hours of talking, I had to realize that it may only ever get as good as that conversation; I would need to resolve, within myself, all the other issues I had with him. A few months after he left, I talked to my then-boyfriend about it, and realized that I had to let it go, or our relationship would just be another lesson I had to learn about my "daddy issues."

As far as who I wanted my dad to be, I also dated guys who I felt would be the dad that I wanted him to be, or rather the dad that I missed. My dad left the household at a pinnacle point, right before high school. For a young girl, that is where things became interesting. My body had already begun to change in middle school, but I started seeing guys differently. I had feelings that I couldn't explain. Thankfully, my mother was an open book when I had questions, but there were just some things I needed Dad for.

Why did guys say they liked me in private, but ignored me in public?

Why does a guy try to date all my friends, and think he'll have a shot with me?

What if I don't want to have sex with a guy, but I'm afraid to lose him?

I could go on all day, but there are certain things that you need a male perspective on, more specifically, your father's perspective. He missed my first date, my first car, my memorable junior Ring Dance, and Prom. These were pivotal times in my adolescence that we couldn't recreate.

I had close girlfriends who would complain about their dads being in their business, or acting like jerks to their boyfriends. Secretly, I wished that were me. My mother was left to play "good cop-bad cop" with my boyfriends. It became confusing to me, but in hindsight, I see why she did it. That scene in *Bad Boys 2,* where Martin and Will interrogate Martin's daughter, stood out to me because she had two men in her life to help shield her from foolishness. While the over-protectiveness could be annoying at times, I envied it. I want to make sure my daughter receives that same rite of passage.

To my sisters out there who weren't raised with a father, I hope and pray that you marry a man who will be the dad that you always dreamed of. For those of you who know your father, while accepting the faults of your dad, try to focus on the traits that were positive. I know it may be difficult, but I truly believe everyone has good in them. I feel, in a sense, that I've had a taste of both worlds, and I have peace in knowing that I was raised with a father in the household for most of my life. For the first 14 years, I had a father who not only came home every night, but who was actively engaged in my life.

One of my favorite memories of my father is that we used to go to McDonald's when they had $.29 Hamburger Day, and we'd take them home and watch "*Martin*," one of my favorite television shows. We would spend countless hours laughing and sitting on the floor of my parents' bedroom, and at that moment, my sister, our father and I were the Three Musketeers. Or I even remember when my dad would take my sister and I to the grocery store to get sherbet, regardless of what time of night it was. Those memories I will keep for a lifetime.

If I could thank my dad for anything, it would be helping me mold the man whom I want to marry. Even if you don't know it, Dad, when you left, you helped me in terms of dating. I knew, because of you, whom I wanted to marry. I knew I wanted someone who would sacrifice for his family, like you did when you entered the military at such a young age. I know you missed out on a lot of your youth, but because of your sacrifice, my sister and I could be raised in an environment much different than you were. We were able to excel in school and really enjoy just being children. I know I emphasized your negative traits, but your thirst for knowledge, history, and education is a trait that I look for in my man. All in all, even though I didn't grow up with you all the way from birth to 18, your presence in my life was always felt.

To my sisters who don't know their dad in any way, shape, or form, I challenge you to be creative. Just like when we were younger, and we would play Barbie's (I know, old school right), we would create Barbie's family and friends, even make up her boyfriend, if you had a Ken doll. I would have the same mind frame here. While it's so unfortunate that your father chose to not be in your life, that doesn't take anything away from you. You are still awesome. You deserve to be loved, and you will be, one day, if you choose. I know it sounds juvenile, but I would create the image that your dad would be, if he were present. I truly believe this will help you in terms of finding a mate.

I think, as women, and especially as little girls, we each know we have one heck of an imagination. We probably still do, if you were to just ask the men we date currently. Why can't we use this same thought process in regard to our fathers? Please understand, I'm not saying ignore the hurt you must feel because your father was not around, or to simply live in dreamland. No. I'm not saying that all. Please go to counseling; talk with someone about your feelings, and if you can't afford counseling, find a friend or family member who can help you.

Recognizing your feelings and addressing them is the first step in recovery, and that step should not be skipped. I do, however, feel that after you have started the healing processing, it could be helpful to create that Dad in your head, and with that, you would know the traits you are looking for in a father, and how you want that father to treat your daughter (if you decide to have children). I think it's worth a try. I think it all helps in thinking positively. The more positive your mind is, the better your life will be.

I would be remiss if I didn't discuss women whose father's were in their life but may have caused so much hurt, anger or abuse that they currently struggle with on a daily basis. Personally, I can't relate to their plight and their struggles. Luckily, I have an amazing friend who has professional experience in this area. Her name is Mary and she is a psychotherapist. Her insight and perspective provides a glimpse into the pain that these women endure daily but also a remedy on how to move past it.

Hi Readers! My name is Mary and I want to thank you for allowing me to interrupt Ericka's story. I have over a decade of experience in psychotherapy services and have a special message for some very special ladies.

So many of you had a father (or grandfather, uncle, step-father, mother's boyfriends) who loved you, respected your right to grow and mature into an independent, strong woman, and protected you from harm. Women who were sexually (physically, mentally, emotionally) abused as children may have had fathers (grandfathers, uncles, step-fathers, mothers' boyfriends) who lusted for them, disrespected all of their boundaries, including their bodies, thoughts, self-concept, freedom, and worth, and only protected them and kept them for their own sick, twisted purposes.

The only difference in the choices each type of woman will make regarding a mate is that one woman makes a choice out of self-respect, confidence, and a powerful, healthy, admirable model of men; the other woman makes a choice out of helplessness, self-doubt, and a powerful, oppressive, selfish, predatory model of men. Girls' fathers do not merely represent "man;" girls' fathers represent "men," just like girls' mothers represent "woman" and "women." That's how it works.

One of my clients, years ago, was a little child of 3 who was sexually molested at the age of 2, by a family "friend," one of two teen-aged, male cousins, who was babysitting her at the time. Turned out, as I engaged in therapy with the little girl, her mother burst into tears and disclosed that something similar had happened to her, when she was a child. In one of the most touching moments I've ever seen, or will see, the little girl rested her head on her mother's shoulder, and put her little arms around her mother's neck, because Mommy was crying.

The point is, in this chapter about how females marry their fathers, the chances are relatively high that a girl who was sexually molested (physically molested, emotionally abused, and/or witnessed domestic violence) will have a view of herself as dirty, worthless, stupid, ugly, only-good-for sex, and helpless to change herself or her circumstances. We see the extremes, sure, in news stories about prostitutes who, at 14, ran away from home to get away from incest, and wound up turning tricks in a faraway, mean, lonely city.

There are a lot of stories like that; and there are also stories about women who were molested as little girls, but established relationships with male partners who were supportive and loving. There's no straight line from being molested by your father and "marrying" your father; there are just high probabilities that abused girls will seek men who will treat them the way they have become accustomed to being treated, based on their early conceptualizations of "man."

A child's brain signals the danger of impending abuse, but the child cannot fight and cannot flee, because the one causing the danger alert (the harm, the pain, the sexual abuse, the physical abuse, the emotional abuse) is one of the grown-ups who have a close relationship with the child. So, no fight; no flight; the child "freezes," or more to the point, the child's natural "fight/flight" brain mechanism hits a horrible snag; it freezes and the child cannot choose anything at all.

The child "freezes" and must submit. So there's more to being sexually abused as a child than just being smaller and weaker than one's abuser; the "more" is that the child functions according to the "freeze" messages from her brain. She has lost her choice of "fight or flight." You can only imagine the effect on that baby's brain of repeated molestation and/or other forms of abuse. Those little brains still function; those children still walk, talk, read, write, jump, dance, and even smile. Their brains do everything other children's brains do; they just don't process information the same way....the safe way. If you cannot trust your brain to alert you when danger is at hand, can you trust any other messages it sends?

Nope.

But it takes some serious work to teach victims of child sexual abuse (and any other form of abuse or exposure to a traumatic event) that their brains are not reliably processing anything. Not the social environment; not the non-verbal messages; not the verbal messages; and not the emotional messages.

Think about it: Have you ever been out with one of your girls, to happy hour, and a guy comes up to the pair of you, and your "gut feeling" is that the guy is a creep from the planet Creepazoid? That's your brain. It's telling you something very important. It is saying, "RUN AWAY OR PUNCH THIS GUY IN HIS UNSHELLED, SALTED PEANUTS!"

What happens if you don't listen to that message? What happens if you can't alert your girl about Creepy Creep, or you alert her, but she shakes you off?

Yeah. I know.

If we seek to marry someone who has qualities, beliefs, and goals that complement, or fit, our own, what kind of man do you think a young woman with a past of sexual abuse looks for?

Right.

She, like you, seeks a man whose qualities complement her own. Her view of what it means to be male is based on early input, just like yours is; it comes from your earliest relationship and interactions with the first male, the most important and influential male, in your life. You might call him, "Dad," but guess what, a woman abused as a child might call him, "Dad," too.

We do what we know to do; we seek what we know to seek; we partner with whom we know to partner, BUT our choices, like the wounds, scars, betrayal, and humiliation that may have occurred to us at the hands of our fathers can affect those choices significantly.

The consequences for women abused as children do not have to be life-long, continued abuse and self-directed negativity. Christ does not want that for them, for you, or for anyone. Finding Christ and accepting His salvation is, in my view, the most beautiful and eloquent choice a woman with an abusive childhood can make. And many do. Knowing that Jesus already suffered the pain of child sexual abuse for you is too awesome and amazing for words. It means you can set it down; you can leave all that pain, fear, blame, shame, and humiliation, and negative, worthless view of yourself at the Cross.

It's been paid for.

God's got this.

In addition, women with abusive childhoods may seek mental health resources for reasons other than having been abused as children, because there is a high likelihood that childhood abuse will go hand-in-hand with depression, anxiety, Post-traumatic Stress Disorder (PTSD), substance abuse, and/or personality disorders. As a psychotherapist who has seen many clients who were victims of childhood abuse, across every spectrum there is, I have had to find a way to remain attentive, to remain receptive to women's stories of childhood abuse, a way to keep a straight face and not dissolve into tears because the words I was hearing broke my own heart and spirit. I have had to keep listening and to keep hearing more, and more, and more about what adults do to children than can fill my lifetime and all of your lifetimes, combined. So here's what I came up with.

Hear me out. As Ericka has said, "don't judge me." Since I cannot grab a very, very sharp knife, and lay in wait for fathers/abusers, and cut off some of their favorite, dangling body parts, I have found an even better way to handle them: I leave it to God!

And here's why: In three of the four gospels, Jesus said essentially the same thing about people who hurt children. First, Christ made clear His view of children. Matthew 19: 13-14: Then were little children presented to him, so that he should impose hands upon them and pray. And the disciples rebuked them. But Jesus said to them:

Suffer the little children, and forbid them not to come to me: for the kingdom of heaven is for such.

Now, "suffer the little children," is the coolest thing I've ever read about parenting, teaching, or any other work that is done with and for children. If God's Son tells *you* to "suffer" the children, He means, "I know it's hard, but put up with them," "they're children, get over it," and my favorite:

"You can threaten (suffer) your child with, 'Just wait until your father hears about this,' but I'm telling you, since I am the Son of God, 'Just wait until MY Father hears about this!'"

But back to the alternative to the sharp knife solution: It's my "One-Word Prayer:" Here it comes:
Dear Lord,
Please, in Jesus' name,
MILLSTONE THAT GUY!
Thank you.
Amen.

Short, to the point, pithy. I recall praying it, and smiling a little, because I had just read a news item about a man who had raped a 24-month-old girl, and had been sentenced to life in prison.

In Texas.

Child molesters are doomed in just about any prison, but Texas prisons are "a whole 'nother hell-on-earth." I gave the guy 36 hours before an "accident" ended his life. Imagine, like I do sometimes, that there is a "Millstone Olympics" in Hell. All the abusive people have to tread burning, boiling water, with heavy stones tied to their necks, forever. FOR-EVER! And listen to elevator music from an elevator they will NEVER ride up!

I've prayed that One-Word Prayer a lot, and urge you to do the same, anytime you witness, or become aware of, a man (or a woman) hurting a child; especially if you were that child.

So what does this have to do with "women who marry their fathers?" Well, the message is, being a woman is being a Child of God. What was done to you matters. It matters a great deal. There is help for you; you are not doomed to having relationships with men who are like your father, or whoever it was that damaged you and hurt you so horribly when you were small and powerless. To get help, find a counselor (probably a woman counselor would be best) whom you can trust, and seek treatment for the consequences of your early abuse. You cannot change what happened; no one can. BUT you can change the way you see yourself; anyone can.

Ericka has just nailed this message; you are loved; you will be loved; you deserve to be loved; and God is the father who will guide you toward the right man. But you can ponder these thoughts, in case you need a reminder,

"And calling to him a child, he put [the child] in the midst of them and said, "Truly, I say to you, unless you turn and become like children, you will never enter the kingdom of heaven. Whoever humbles himself like this child is the greatest in the kingdom of heaven. "Whoever receives one such child in my name receives me, but whoever causes one of these little ones who believe in me to sin, it would be better for him to have a great millstone fastened around his neck and to be drowned in the depth of the sea. (Matthew 18:2-6 ESV)

"See that you do not despise one of these little ones. For I tell you that in heaven their angels always see the face of my Father who is in heaven. (Matthew 18:10 ESV)

"It is impossible that scandals should not come, but woe to him through whom they come. It were better for him that a millstone were hanged about his neck, and he cast into the sea, than that he should scandalize one of these little ones." (Luke 17:1-2)

"And whosoever shall scandalize one of these little ones that believe in me; it were better for him that a millstone were hanged about his neck, and he were cast into the sea."(Mark 9:41-42)

I hope you enjoyed Mary's message and her "sweet" sense of humor. I pray her words encouraged you to realize you are worth and most importantly are deserving of the best. God paid the ultimate price for your wounds and while I can't understand the pain you have endured, Christ does.

You can't help that your dad isn't a part of your life or he was and hurt you whether emotionally, physically or sexually. You can't help that you had to figure out how to date and who to marry without your father's input, or that you will suffer heartache that could have been avoided, had your father been actively in your life.

What you can help is the future that is in front of you. If you use your circumstances to dictate your future, you can probably count on your future dictating your past. Your mind is a battlefield, and the mines that cause explosions are the negative thoughts. Retraining your mind is hard, but necessary for growth and thriving.

During the last few years of my dad living with the family, he started to stay away for days at a time. I would often worry, thinking something might have happened to him, and I would have anxiety until he returned. That would sometimes go on for days. It was no way for a child to live. My sister and I would then worry about our mom. If she were two minutes late in getting home, we would automatically think something happened to her, too.

That kind of hyper-vigilance continued in my relationships. When my boyfriend was late, or didn't answer the phone, I would immediately think the worst. I'm sure I stressed out a few of them. I would often say, because of my dad, x, y, and z. I felt I had a reason to worry, and they should just accept that. I didn't realize I was letting my past experiences dictate my future.

After many years of worrying, I went to church and heard the pastor say, "If you are going to worry, don't pray and if you are going to pray, don't worry." I've heard that many times, and in many different ways, but for some reason, that time, it stuck with me. I realized I had to make a change, and that the stress was affecting my body. I would get chest pains that would come randomly.

Your mental and emotional health is related to your physical health, and I knew, if I wanted to stay healthy, I would need to make some adjustments. I am still training my mind not to think of the worst, and while I do sometimes, I have made great strides in the last few years. Training your mind is not easy, but it is so worth it. I ask you to train your mind to think positively. Know your future is bright, and that despite the love you may not have received as a child or adolescent, the love you do deserve is waiting for you, and you have the capacity to receive it all.

Chapter 17
Can We Talk?

It's been nearly a year since RJ and I last spoke. While that was surprising to many, it was routine for me. As much as I was a little unnerved that he didn't call or text on my birthday that had passed a few months ago, how could I blame him? After all, I didn't reach out to him either.

That all changed, one night in December. RJ's mother sent me a text on the second night I was in Boston, attending a leadership conference. The text was simple, but the last sentence was all I needed to see, "Just know you are always in my heart." Even if it was from his mother, and not him, it was nice to know that I was thought about when I felt like I had been a distant memory to him and his family.

Let's be real, I pretty much took it as his feelings, whether I had proof or not. See, RJ's mother and I were close, especially in the short amount of time that RJ and I were dating and were engaged. Growing up, I remember seeing her around, but I never had an opportunity to sit down and talk to her. Like my mom, she worked hard to raise her children, and sometimes, she had to do it alone. Once RJ and I reconnected, his mom and I clicked instantly, and would email each other for hours, almost every day. We would discuss everything, from our favorite colors, our favorite scriptures, and the hopes and desires we had for our families and ourselves.

One of the hardest parts of breaking off my engagement was breaking up with RJ's momma. Society leads us to believe that you have to watch out for in-laws, because they are always in your business, or don't think you are good enough for their son/daughter. It was the exact opposite for me. She was very candid about her son, and she seemed to love the fact that I knew him well enough to love him, but not let him get away with much. She was truly like another mother to me, and it angered me, knowing that we wouldn't be able to be as close anymore.

I know some of you may think that you can still call your ex's family members, whether it's a mother, sister, or cousin, after the relationship has ended. I'm here to tell you, you may want to reconsider that notion. As much as I loved her, I knew that we would have to break up, too, if I was to move on with someone else and establish a relationship with his mother.

I knew I would compare the two, and ultimately, either be back with my RJ because of the relationship, or question his mother to see what he's up to. Both are unhealthy, and I would advise you against it. If you don't trust me, try it out, and if it works for you, you should be the one to write a book about it.

I do need to note that, if you have children, this doesn't apply to you. Those relationships will go on for a lifetime and, because of those children, those relationships cannot, or should not, be severed just because your part of the relationship is over.

For those of you who have pets, you just may need a mediator.

Needless to say, after I responded to RJ's mother, I get a text from RJ a few hours later. His text seemed familiar, almost as if we had been talking this whole time.

"Hey McCracken...I'd like to call you tomorrow. Would that be ok with you?" He had to be kidding me, right? So almost a whole year goes by and now you want to talk?

When I read that, as happy I was to know that at least two people in his family remembered me, I wondered, "Why now, and why did I have to hear from your mother first?" I decided I had some things to get off of my chest, so why not? My boyfriend at the time knew a great deal about RJ's and my history, and he was fine with me asking the questions that I had not had the opportunity to ask in the last year.

Fast forward to later that evening. I tell RJ I'm free and he calls. Was I nervous? A little, but was I ready, absolutely!

The voice sounds the same, I thought, as he spoke. I

can tell he is nervous because he keeps clearing his throat, but he starts off with general conversation.

"How are you? How was your day?"

I play this game for a few minutes, and then finally ask what he wants to talk about. I'm very nice, but direct. He can notice that, so he begins to clear his throat once more. Finally, he says he wants us to be friends.

Friends.

Really?

I did not know what friends looked like with a guy that I agreed to marry, but didn't. After that, I didn't hear much of what else he said, but I knew I had a few things to get off my chest.

I asked EVERY question I had been thinking about over that last year!

You would have thought he was being interrogated on *The First 48,* the way I rattled off those questions.

Ladies, if you ever get the opportunity to ask your

ex questions about your relationship, please remember to be calm and gentle. Gentleness will get you authentic answers, while anger, hurt, and frustration will get you the answers that your ex may think you want to hear. I realized later that I was thankful to have had the necessary time, not only to evaluate a multitude of things I wanted to say, but I realized, overall, I was less angry and combative. Had we had that conversation a month after the engagement was over, or even 6 months later, I believe the anger would have been unmistakable, and I may not have received the genuine answers I needed. I'm so thankful to God and His timing.

After my tirade of questions, I proceeded with the main one: "Why did you propose so fast in the first place?"

He responded very honestly. He knew that I was the one, but he felt he had to capture that opportunity immediately, or else I might have been dating someone else, and he would not have the chance. The relationship I was in before him scared him a bit, because he thought I would actually marry the guy. He also wanted me to be with him in LA, and knew the only way I would move was to be married. Even though his decision at that time caused more heartache and pain than I thought I would be able to handle, I appreciated his honesty. I was in a better place to receive it.

After all the questions were answered, we were right back into friend mode. We updated each other on what had transpired in the last year, leaving our love lives out of it. We laughed and joked, and it felt like we hadn't skipped a beat. It was almost eerie.

How could someone that hurt me so much in the last year make me laugh this soon? I didn't fight it, but I still had my guard up. After about two hours of conversing, we ended our conversation, but the question still remained, could we be friends? I wasn't sure just yet, so I told him, if he called, and I wanted to answer, I would, and if didn't, I wouldn't. Until I understood what this friendship was going to look like, I couldn't give him an answer, one way or the other.

I knew, after we got off the phone, I not only felt peace, but I also felt empowerment. Things were on my

223

terms now. I could live with that.

I informed my boyfriend at the time, and he was supportive as usual. To be honest, our relationship was coming to a close, so I'm not sure if he would have said much else. I grew a lot during our relationship, and I was thankful for the time we spent, but felt that, ultimately, we were in two separate phases in life. He was rebuilding a lot of things in life, due to decisions he made when he was younger, and I felt that I wanted to move forward with my family, and we just were not compatible at that juncture.

It was painful, but very necessary. Our season was up, but I'm so thankful for what he taught me, and I pray I left him better than when I entered his life. The next few weeks passed, and besides a text from RJ to check in, communication was limited, and not initiated by myself.

I think that when you endure such heartache, you have to make sure to guard your heart with everything you have. As easy as it was for me to slip back into best friend mode, I had to remember when to pull back. That was unnatural, especially for someone I had known half of my life, but it was necessary to avoid heartache again. Until you can gain full trust in that person, don't allow yourself to slip too soon back into old habits of talking and texting every day. It could cause you more heartache and confusion in the end, if boundaries are not established.

By mid-January, I was in Washington, DC for training, while my family and friends in Atlanta were reeling from a recent ice storm. Who knew two inches of ice could cause so much havoc? Thankfully, everyone I knew was safe and sound at home, waiting for the ice to melt. Meanwhile, back in DC, I was doing what most Washingtonians did, hitting up Happy Hour. I met with so many friends from back home, and I was excited, because in a few short months, DC would be my home for three months.

The last day of my trip, I was up early, packing my bags and getting ready to head downstairs for breakfast, when I received a text from my RJ. It had to be about 6:45 am Eastern, which meant it was ridiculously early on the West Coast. The text was simple, "Hey there. If you happen to be awake, would you be willing to call me?"

Immediately, I called him, assuming someone was hurt or sick, or planning a funeral. What else would he want to talk about that early?

Of course, he hit me with the small talk initially, like our previous conversation.

"What's up?" I quickly stated.

This call was standing between myself and my made-to-order omelet that awaited me downstairs. RJ took a deep breath, and then he went into how he knew he made a mistake, and how he'd been thinking about it for a while. To be honest, after I heard the first few words, I realized where this was going. I sat down, square in the middle of my bed, and put my hand across my forehead. I didn't know what to feel at the time.

Vindication?

Happiness?

Anger?

I was all over the place. I let him talk for a few more minutes, and then I told him I had to go. I walked downstairs and confided what had just happened to my co-worker. She looked happy, and continued to boost my confidence by saying that she was glad he realized what a gem she already knew I was. Honestly, that didn't make me feel any less confused. I still didn't know what to do.

The rest of day was a blur. I attended the rest of the conference I was there for, but I wasn't present mentally. I hugged my co-workers goodbye, but wasn't sure what was awaiting me, once I got home.

By the time I arrived at the airport, I called someone who I knew would be able to give me wisdom and sound advice. One of my sorority sisters had gone through something similar, and her ex-beau had just made a similar declaration that he wanted to re-enter her life again, about two months prior. She was stunned when I told her what happened, and I knew why. We've usually gone through the same situation at different times. We have been able to lean on each other, usually because we've been there. In the last four years, we had consistently leaned on each other during relationship troubles, because usually, one of us had just gone through it and could offer insight. She didn't scold me for considering allowing him back in my life, but she cautioned me to ensure I laid the ground rules first, and set parameters that he had to meet. I knew I couldn't allow him to just walk back in my life, without regaining my trust, as well as the trust of those who supported me, throughout the ordeal. It had been mandatory for her ex to meet with her mother, the person who consoled her when he broke her heart. At 6'4", two hundred odd pounds, he had to meet her 5'2", one hundred and forty pound mother. He had to face her, and not only apologize to her, but explain why he deserved a second chance.

Genius I thought.

I decided to adopt the same plan, and was ready to give him an earful, once we spoke again.

On the plane ride home, I slept, and once I awoke, I was ready to face this thing, head on. I called him, and immediately, he apologized, on hearing that I had a boyfriend. To be honest, it made me think that, once again, he was only thinking about himself.

How could he not ask me about my relationship status before he made such a declaration? Regardless of the fact that my current relationship was nearing a close, RJ had no idea of that. What kind of position would that put me in? I accepted his apology but kept him at bay.

I needed to see changes, and the year we were apart, I hoped some things had sunk in, such as priorities of career and family, as well as him being a man of his word. I wasn't sure if it had sunk in, at that point. I began to tell him what I needed, and it was a lot.

I believe, when you are in the seat to make a decision of whether to take back the man who broke your heart, stomped on it, and then rode a bike over it, you should be pretty clear on your expectations. Regardless of whether I was going to take him back or not, he needed to know what my standards were at that point.

The past year gave me the opportunity to understand what I needed in a mate, and I wanted RJ to be clear on that. I prided myself for so long, in being the reliable girlfriend who was there when you needed her.

I could cook, clean, and update your resume, without batting an eye.

I listened to your dreams and comforted you during your trials.

I felt like I knew what it was to be a wife. I only had one question: Who was going to be there for me?

Superwoman syndrome is real, and I could be cast for the part, along with a bunch of other women I know. I focused so much on what it was to be a great wife, that I didn't consider what kind of husband I would need to support me. Of course, he has to have a relationship with God, he has to have ambition, and he has to be a provider.

What about someone with whom I could be vulnerable? Someone who knew that I don't always have it together, and who will hang up my "cape" for me, when I am dog tired.

Someone who would nurture my dreams and elevate me to the next level, with his love and confidence in me.

Someone who would allow me to take off my "thinking cap," and then take the lead, without me even having to ask. Someone who would pray, with and for me, when I couldn't find the words.

This is the husband that not only I desired, but the one I will have someday. I told RJ I needed time to think about everything he said, but he better think about what I just said, as well, if wanted any kind of shot at being with me.

I felt so confident about my talk with RJ that I did not even go home after I landed. I knew I needed to confide in someone about all that had transpired within the last twelve hours. I met up at a local cafe with one of my closest girlfriends, and you wouldn't even begin to guess who came through the door, my ex-boyfriend. His grin was so wide, I believed his eyes disappeared and he showed every tooth he had. I felt bad, because I knew that he was hoping we could reconcile, but after the latest happening, I couldn't. Not just because of RJ, but because I realized that, as awesome as he was, he wasn't the mate God destined for me.

I smiled and told him I would talk to him later, after a few minutes of casual conversation. I knew that the next talk with my ex-boyfriend would be one of our last, but I had no time to focus on that right then. I had a decision to make, and I knew I needed a clear head.

When I thought about who could give me the best advice, I immediately thought about our pre-marital counselor. I hadn't spoken to him in nearly a year, either. One of the last things he relayed to me, when I told him about RJ's and my engagement being up in the air, was that I would be ok. He told me RJ would one day regret this, but to just know that I was going to be ok. Honestly, I didn't believe him when he told me RJ would regret this. I felt that because he felt so strongly that we wouldn't work out, and he was the catalyst in ending the engagement, how could he go back on that? How could I consider taking him back?

At that point, I needed Godly insight. Besides that, our pre-marital counselor knew the ins-and-outs of the relationship, and would provide non-biased recommendations. The only problem was, he had left the church I attended and I didn't have any way to contact him. That is, until I remembered that everybody, their mother and their newborn baby, were on Facebook. I wasn't sure if he even remembered me, but I figured it was worth a try. My friend encouraged me to look him up, and what do you know, his profile picture was staring at me like, "How could you think I wouldn't be up here." I was elated, but a little nervous to send him a message.

I soon realized I had no time to second-guess myself. I just had to do it. This decision was too important. The worst that could happen would be that he would not respond. Luckily, my friend was there to push me to do it. I might not have had the courage to do it, if I had been by myself. I had a million reasons why I shouldn't, and only one reason why I should. I had nowhere else to turn.

Honoring God was what brought me to him, so why shouldn't I see if the minister could help, I began to ponder. With trembling fingers, I sent him a message, and squinted my eyes, but within seconds, he answered.

Won't God do it?!

He told me he could talk when I was free, and I made an appointment for the following week. I was happy, but sad, perplexed, but hopeful. I was a ball full of emotions, but I felt like I finally had control. The ball was in my court and I knew I had to devise my next move, carefully and with tons of prayer.

RJ and I talked intermittently for the next few weeks, while I was still in decision-making mode. I felt like I was making strides and, all in all, I had peace. Regardless of what decision I made, I was happy that we were able to talk about everything that happened, and that I could tell him not only how much he hurt me, but also that I had finally forgiven him.

I only had one other person to convince that, not only was I ok, but that I also would make the best decision for me. My sister. My twin sister that is. Growing up, I had always been the more aggressive one, and my sister had been the more passive one. Well, as we grew up, the roles reversed. My sister didn't play when it came to her family, especially her husband and her twin. She was there from the beginning, and even gave RJ her blessing to propose.

234

She felt somewhat responsible for my pain, and didn't want to hear his name again. Ever.

When I told my sister about his call, she was upset. She wanted to know what he wanted, and why now. She had no sympathy, and was very adamant that this was not a good idea. I knew how she felt, and respected it, but I couldn't live for her. You have to remember, while you may not be upset anymore, the people who wiped your tears, rubbed your back, or destroyed his stuff, aren't going to be as happy as you are that your ex is trying to come back into your life.

You can choose to not talk with your friends and family about your feelings, but it could cause a rift. For a few weeks, I dodged ever bringing up the subject of RJ at all, but it all came to a head one Saturday afternoon. The day before, my sister had actually brought up RJ, and she had begun crying because she felt I would just let him back in, despite all the pain he had caused me, and those who supported me. I consoled her, just as she consoled me for the months after the engagement ended, but I was a bit annoyed, to be honest. I felt, once again, I had to think about others, when at this point, I wanted to focus on my feelings and what I wanted and needed.

I had an indescribable peace that couldn't be explained, despite everything that was happening around me, and I needed my sister to understand that. I couldn't give anyone the peace I had. I was hoping that it would be the last conversation about that matter. I was sadly mistaken.

Saturday afternoon. My sister and her sister-in-law came over to my home so that we could go shopping together. We stopped at a few stores within the next few hours, but I felt like I should tell my sister's sister-in-law about RJ, if only for the fact that he re-emerged. I couldn't find the right time, because I didn't want to bring it up in front of my sister again, knowing her feelings behind it. I did what any normal person would do, I waited until my sister ran in the store for a few seconds, and then I said it so quickly, I wasn't even sure if she understood what I said or not.

Remember those, *"We had a baby, it's a boy"* Geico commercials? Same concept. She looked puzzled, once I mumbled the news, but I had no more time to explain at the present moment. We stopped at another store, and by the time we made it to the local Ikea parking lot, my sister's sister-in-law told everything. She revealed that both of us had told her about RJ, and both of us told her not to tell each other. I thought it was funny. My twin, not so much. She told me, once again, how she wanted more answers why her sister-in-law offered more advice.

By that time, I'd had enough. I could feel my eyes welling with tears, and my hands began to shake. I didn't want to do this now, but it looked like I had no choice. I told them both that, unless they had a scripture to give me, I didn't want their advice. All I needed from them, at that point, was prayer, and lots of it. For a moment, I couldn't hear much. They both sat there, and finally agreed. We hugged it out, and finally, walked into Ikea. I knew that I had a road in front of me, and with my family's support or not, this was a journey I had to take on my own.

That situation taught me that while I had forgiven RJ, those who supported me during that difficult time didn't share my sentiments. While they may have forgiven him, that didn't mean that they wanted me to have any contact with him anymore. My twin remembered, vividly, all the pain that I endured; she didn't want me to have to go through that again. I had to respect that. I had to understand that. That didn't mean I was going to go along with what she wanted, but I had to understand her perspective and the validity of it.

Despite how my sister's comments made me feel, she had a right to express them, and I needed to be there for her. She was scared and nervous for me, and just did not want my emotions and feelings to over-cloud my better judgment. I couldn't for a second believe that; just because I had accepted him back in my life in some capacity, she had to, as well.

RJ and I spoke quite frequently in the following weeks, and he even came to visit me in Atlanta soon after. Our trip was cut short because I had to go out of town for work at the last minute, but once I saw him, I felt peace.

Time had passed, but our feelings for each other had not changed. The love was still there, and at that point, I wasn't sure if it ever left.

After RJ's visit, we spoke daily. We talked about life, our dreams, and our individual aspirations, but there was not a lot of talk about what to do about our relationship. We were still across the country from each other, and neither one of us wanted to move.

By this time, six months had already passed, and I was already in DC. I enjoyed being close to family, since I'm from Virginia, but I still didn't feel like RJ and I had made much progress in our relationship. I informed him, when he initially called, he needed a plan to be with me, and I had yet to receive one. Things were too comfortable, exactly as I had feared. I knew, at that point, in order for me to move forward, with or without him, I would have to disrupt the comfort.

About three weeks later, I asked RJ what his plans were for me, and he was very general. Marriage and family were indeed at the top of the list, but there was no clear intent on how to get there. Feeling like I was going to get trapped again, I told him I wanted us to date other people, since he had nothing specific on how we would be united. Seems dumb, if I really only wanted to date him, but I felt like he owed it to me, to show me that he wanted me this time. If he couldn't, I would have to move on, even if I had to force myself. Despite not dating one person over the next six weeks, I was proud of myself for the declaration, and prayerful for RJ to feel the pressure and really commit to this relationship and me.

Little did I know, this was all wrong!

I was not exhibiting faith.

I didn't want to lose him completely, so I decided that this declaration would bring us closer.

I didn't trust God enough to walk away completely, so I thought that I could still hold on, somewhat, but somehow still have the upper hand.

Tsk tsk tsk. Little did I know I would win the battle, but not the war.

At about the end of the next six weeks, RJ told me something I thought I would never hear him say. He was considering moving to Atlanta. This was a huge deal for me, considering his sentiments for needing to stay in LA for his career. At that moment, I truly felt that God answered my prayers. I wanted us to be together, and for him to say that he was the one considering moving, because of the quality of life Atlanta would bring him, in regard to being closer to family, and the great cost of living, it was a no-brainer to me.

I didn't press him on this new revelation immediately. After a few days, I asked him, was he still feeling the same way, and what timeframe was he looking at. RJ responded that he wanted to move within a year after he had made more connections in LA, and had found employment in Atlanta.

After nearly seven years of going back and forth, what was another year I thought? RJ was even proactive in this move, by updating his resume and looking for virtual jobs. I was so excited, yet so fearful, that he would change his mind. It was an extreme mix of emotions that I tried to handle.

After my return to Atlanta, after my summer in DC, I was more excited than ever. Not only was I back in my own home, but I was subconsciously preparing it for RJ to be here. I thought about closet and drawer space, even though it would be a year before he would be there, and frankly, I had no idea when he would move in, because he was going to get his own place until we were married.

I wanted things to be perfect, even though, in my gut, I wasn't sure if his move would come into fruition. Despite the plan RJ had finally given me, I wasn't sure if he were being genuine, or if this was just a way to keep me in his life. I tried not to let those thought sway me, but they eventually came to a head a few weeks later.

RJ informed me that he still planned on coming to Atlanta, but he wasn't sure of a date.
Huh?

He kept trying to reassure me that he was still coming, but now, only 3 months after declaring this move, he was talking himself out of it. I didn't know what to do. I would love to say I was completely shocked, but I wasn't. More hurt than anything else.

Was this déjà vu?

Why was this happening again?

My birthday was in two weeks, and the tickets had already been purchased, so I decided to hold my peace until he got here. I didn't want to spend my birthday weekend possibly ending my relationship with him, but this time, I wanted to look him in the eye when we had the conversation.

My birthday was great, and we both acted as if this huge elephant in the room was not there, until the night before he left. As we sat facing each other on the couch, the same couch where I sat when I ended the engagement, I asked him what his intentions were, and told him how much I needed his specific plans to feel secure in our relationship. He understood why I needed the plan, but stated plainly that he couldn't provide it to me.

I knew, right at that moment, that the relationship was over, but I didn't want his last night to be remembered in such a way, so we both decided to revisit it later, and enjoy our last few hours together.

That next morning, I took him to the airport, while in my mind I believed this might be the last time I would see him. I dabbed my eyes as I drove away, and remember, distinctly, RJ giving me one last glance before he checked his bags.

Oddly, another two weeks went by, and our schedules were so busy that we didn't have much time to revisit that last conversation. As the second week came to a close, I knew I had to talk to him, and to finally accept that, with no plan, we couldn't continue.

That night, he would call when he got off work, and I would once again ask him, did he have a plan, accepting that nothing had changed. It was then I told him I could no longer be with him, because of the uncertainty of our future. Thinking, this time, he would jump in and say what I always wanted him to say.

"I can't lose you again. Let's work this out."

Instead, he said nothing. Just as before, but this time I was prepared. We hung up the phone, and once again, I felt deserted, but somehow empowered. I made a decision that I deserved more, and would require it, even if the outcome was not what I desired.

After a break up, as we all know, we go through a range of emotions. I went from empowered to sad. From sad to confused. From confused to angry. However, this time, the anger was more with myself.

How could I have gotten myself so invested, this time around, and with no plan? Why did I even entertain a relationship with him again? These questions flooded my mind constantly, and caused a major shift in my mood. I didn't maintain my joy, the joy that I had pledged to keep throughout this whole ordeal.

As I took a bathroom break at work, the week following the breakup, I ran into a fellow colleague. We exchanged our usual hellos and how is your day going. I don't know how we got on the subject, but she told me about a book she was trying to finish, that she had been working on for several years. I told her I was currently completing my book, too, and she inquired about the subject matter. I gave her the background on myself and of my and RJ's story, and why I decided to share my experience. Unbeknownst to me, she had been engaged before and broke it off five weeks before the wedding. She shared her story about the peace she didn't have throughout the whole process and how the disrespect of his mother led her to call it off, knowing her fiancé, at the time, had a hand in the matter. I was intrigued by her candidness, because we were very surface level friends, more so, strict colleagues, but I knew God sent her to me that day. We ended up talking for a few hours, and while I thought I had found an ally because of her engagement story, I was shocked by what she revealed to me.

After listening to me rant about RJ's lack of consistency, and how he made me feel that I always came second to his career, she informed that I hadn't quite let him go because of the resentment I still had towards him. In her words, I had not honored the love we shared, despite the outcome. I had not left the situation in a good place. I was belligerent in how I broke things off, but it wasn't done out of love, but out of frustration. She informed me that I would need to call RJ back and end things the "right way," the loving way, if I wanted to fully move on from him. As we both cried in her office, she told me that I reminded her of a younger version of herself, and she didn't want me to make the same mistakes she had made.

"Your love is right there, Ericka, but you've got to do this. You have to leave the relationship in an honorable way."

Through my tears, I knew she was right. I didn't want his last impression of me to be short, cold, and emotionless. I wanted RJ to know that I loved him, but couldn't stay in a relationship that wasn't serving me. I called RJ that evening and scheduled to speak with him two days later. He was a bit confused and annoyed that I didn't just tell him what I needed to say that day, but I knew I was too raw with emotion. I had to settle my thoughts and, this time, verbalize them out of love.

It was ten o'clock Eastern when RJ actually called me. I could tell he really wanted to hear what I had to say, and I was finally ready to let it out.

"RJ, I felt that when we talked last time, my frustration got the best of me, and I want you to know that I do not hate you, or even dislike you. I am just upset about how things ended. I will get over it, but I want you to know that I genuinely want the best for you, as a friend should."

To be honest, RJ seemed a little annoyed because that was all I had to say.

"I know you don't hate me, and I would never see you in a negative light," he replied.

Even though he didn't think it was deserved, I knew I had to say it. I had to let him go, but this time with love, peace, and faith that what God has for me is truly for me. I didn't have to hold on to RJ, afraid he would get things together in time for another woman to benefit from it. I realized that it wasn't faith, but fear, that had kept me with him for nearly the last year.

I thought I had given this relationship to God once RJ called to profess his love. I realized, at that moment, that by letting him go, I was actually releasing the love that I desired and deserved to come to me.

The next man who wins my heart will have to prove himself, not only to me, but to God, that he is worthy. Proverbs 18:22 states, "Whoso findeth a wife findeth a good thing, and obtaineth favour of the LORD." My heart is so buried in God now that the man I marry will have to seek Him deeply enough to find it. I know now, more than ever, that God protects his children, especially His daughters, and He will continue to do so. The husband He has for me will not be perfect, but will be imperfectly made for me. If it's RJ, we will have an incredible story of love and forgiveness. If it's someone else, RJ's and my relationship has given me the tools essential to be a great wife.

I leave with you a few signs to beware of, in regard to your ex-fiancé and your future.

1.   **Beware** of old feelings. It's normal to revert back, SOMETIMES, to that hurt you felt. Recognize, when you do, so you can do it less often.

2.   **Beware** of old behaviors- If you notice patterns of behavior that caused your relationship to falter initially, ensure that, if you see them again, you address them quickly, or dismiss your ex speedily. Learn your lesson as soon as possible, so you can go on to the next.

3.   **Beware** of God's grace and mercy- Regardless of where you are in life, God has a plan that is better than you could ever craft for yourself. Keep Him in the driver's seat and remember, He doesn't need your help navigating.

Romans 8:28 says: "And we know that all things work together for good to them that love God, to them who are called according to His purpose." My actions purposed me to endure this heartache to help others, to either avoid this pain, or to help them emerge from it. Your ALTARcation doesn't mean you won't make it to the altar, just that your journey will be different. As I continue to work on myself to be the wife and mother that is deserving of great love and adoration, I charge you to do the same.

You are more than an unsuccessful engagement, and you are even more than what you have experienced. Keep praying, hoping, believing, and working towards the love that you so desire, because ultimately, what doesn't kill you makes you more than a "conqueror.

Reference List:

Osteen, Joel. *Your Best Life Now: 7 Steps to Living at Your Full Potential*. New York: Warner, 2004. Print.

Schlessinger, Laura. *Bad Childhood, Good Life: How to Blossom and Thrive in Spite of an Unhappy Childhood*. New York: Harper Collins Publishers, 2006. Print.

Merriam-Webster. Merriam-Webster. Web. 10 Feb. 2015. <http://www.merriam-webster.com/>

About the Author

Ericka McCracken has been writing ever since she can remember. She majored in English as an undergraduate student, but she never imagined that one day she would be completing her very own memoir. Her first book, ALTARcation, promises to be a book that will not only be inspirational but will challenge you to forgive those who have hurt you, including yourself.

Ericka currently resides in Atlanta, Georgia